SUCCESSFUL ACQUISITIONS

A Proven Plan for Strategic Growth

David Braun

AMACOM

AMERICAN MANAGEMENT ASSOCIATION

New York • Atlanta • Brussels • Chicago • Mexico City • San Francisco
Shanghai • Tokyo • Toronto • Washington, D.C.

Bulk discounts available. For details visit:
www.amacombooks.org/go/specialsales
Or contact special sales:
Phone: 800-250-5308
E-mail: specialsls@amanet.org
View all the AMACOM titles at: www.amacombooks.org
American Management Association: www.amanet.org

This publication is designed to provide accurate and authoritative information in regard to the subject matter covered. It is sold with the understanding that the publisher is not engaged in rendering legal, accounting, or other professional service. If legal advice or other expert assistance is required, the services of a competent professional person should be sought.

Library of Congress Cataloging-in-Publication Data

Braun, David, 1965-
    Successful acquisitions : a proven plan for strategic growth / David Braun.
      pages cm
    Includes bibliographical references and index.
    ISBN-13: 978-0-8144-3265-5 (hbk.)
    ISBN-10: 0-8144-3265-4 (hbk.)
1. Consolidation and merger of corporations.   I. Title.
HD2746.5.B737   2013
658.1'62—dc23

                                                              2012045578

About AMA

American Management Association (www.amanet.org) is a world leader in talent development, advancing the skills of individuals to drive business success. Our mission is to support the goals of individuals and organizations through a complete range of products and services, including classroom and virtual seminars, webcasts, webinars, podcasts, conferences, corporate and government solutions, business books, and research. AMA's approach to improving performance combines experiential learning—learning through doing—with opportunities for ongoing professional growth at every step of one's career journey.

Printing number

10 9 8 7 6 5 4 3 2 1

Dedication

To my always-supportive wife Karen and daughters Krista and Ingrid.

Acknowledgments

I am most appreciative of the creative work Jon Ward did to help transform my ideas and thoughts into something people would actually want to read. He is truly a gifted craftsman with writing. Thank you to Matt Craft for his many hours of videotaping, drafting, editing, and pulling it all together, a yeoman's job well done. Finally a special note to the late Dr. Jim Hudick, a scholarly practice leader from the American Management Association, who inspired me to write this book many years ago when he asked, "How does all this M&A stuff work—can you draw it out for me on the board?" That's what led to the Roadmap you will find in these pages.

CONTENTS

PART 3: BUILD THE DEAL

INTRODUCTION:
FROM BEGINNING
TO BEGINNING

I WAS CLOSE to getting the deal. The lawyers were fretting, but that's what they are paid for. Our due diligence was producing mountains of complex data, but that's normal. And George, my acquisition-hungry client, was excited. He had the gleam in his eye of a connoisseur who had stumbled on a rare diamond, and he was ready to grab the trophy.

There was a problem, though. In his enthusiasm, George was getting pushy. "How low will they go?" was his mantra. For him, every transaction was about the price and nothing but the price. Meanwhile, Anthony, the seller, was stalling on the numbers.

They were a study in contrast, these two. George was a relentless type-A entrepreneur. Not yet forty, he'd built three successful companies and had an insatiable appetite for work, fast cars, and business growth. Anthony, the seller, was in his early seventies. A man of few words, he drove a beat-up Chevy truck that belied a lifetime of steady achievement. Anthony had started life in the stockroom and ended up buying out his employer. Over some thirty years, he had quietly built a tiny local supply store into a $20 million debt-free enterprise.

I didn't know what the exact problem was, but I did know that George was making a mistake. When it comes to buying companies, especially privately held ones, the transaction is almost never about just the price. There is always something going on that falls outside the spreadsheets. Understanding that mysterious "something" is often what makes or breaks the deal.

The statistics are frightening. By most reckonings, 77 percent of company acquisitions fail to deliver expected outcomes. George's deal was heading in that direction, and I was determined to save him from himself.

I sent my research team back into the field to find out more about Anthony. You can never know too much about a seller, and although we had a pretty good picture of his business history and financial situation, I knew there was a missing piece. Anthony seemed to have everything. He lived on a fifty-acre ranch, and I knew he had invested well in the stock market. There was nothing about his financial picture that would cause him to worry about this sale. So what was it? All I had noticed was that there was something sad about the guy.

"Do you know that Anthony starts work at 6:30 every morning?" my researcher reported. "He unlocks the building, stays later than any of his fifty employees, and he closes the place up again at night." For a business owner of seventy-three, that seemed odd.

I decided to invite Anthony to dinner and chat with him about everything except the deal. I wanted to gently break through his reserve and find out more about the man behind the mask. For an hour, we conversed about this and that, with me doing most of the talking just to get him relaxed. Then, over coffee, he suddenly opened up and told me his story.

Anthony had married late in life, and this unexpected union brought him renewed happiness. He immediately started making plans to withdraw from the business so he could travel the world with his wife. Tragically, she died of a stroke within two years of their marriage. Her two sons from a previous marriage wanted nothing to do with Anthony. In fact, they fought him over money they wrongly believed they should be inheriting.

The business was all Anthony had left in the world. He knew he would soon be too old to run it effectively, and that's why he was selling. At the same time, he just couldn't tear himself away. He had no problem with the price, although that's what it looked like on the surface. He was stalling for one simple reason. In selling the company, he was confronting a gaping void in his life.

The next day, I met with George. I told him he could get the deal at the price he wanted, but he had to make an adjustment to the agreement.

"We have to find a place for Anthony in the company," I said. "Something where he can contribute his wisdom and experience, without holding back the changes you want to make."

George was amazed.

"He's over seventy! Why doesn't he just retire?"

I chuckled.

"Why don't you?" I asked the restless young multimillionaire.

George took the point, and he appointed Anthony vice president of operational development, a post where he could use his expertise to continually improve the company's systems. The title prompted Anthony to raise a slightly mocking smile, but at least it was a smile. And the deal closed that month.

WHY THIS BOOK IS NEEDED

I am making one simple assumption in this book—that you want to grow your business. But what happens when growth hits a ceiling? When current markets are saturated? When existing product lines are exhausted? When there just seems no way to expand, however hard you push? My purpose in these pages is to give you a breakthrough solution—a complete roadmap to successful expansion through acquiring other companies.

Beyond that, I want to help you expand your understanding of mergers and acquisitions, of how they unfold in the real world, especially for the mid-market player.

For most people, M&A has a peculiar aura. On the one hand, there's an unmistakable fascination in the spectacle of massive corporations eating each other alive. On the other hand, most M&A literature comes in the form of heavy academic tomes, packed with legalese and financial equations of little use to the average businessperson. It seems the subject is simultaneously glamorous and impenetrably dull. In this book, I will show you a world of M&A that is both fascinating and accessible.

First, a reality check. Most acquisitions are not multi-billion-dollar takeovers. According to Bloomberg's M&A Advisory League Tables (April 2, 2012), 97 percent of all M&A transactions are below $500 million in value. That means that every year, hundreds of amicable transactions are consummated between modest-sized companies, the majority of which are privately owned. You rarely read about these deals in the business press, and by definition, a private transaction yields less public information. Yet this activity is absolutely essential to a healthy economy.

This book is different from most others on mergers and acquisitions, because it is focused exclusively on the small to mid-market sector, where most M&A activity actually occurs. And it is entirely concerned with the art of buying. Most important, what you will find here is a practical step-by-step plan for acquisition based on fundamental principles. Every detail of the plan has been tested and proven through decades of overseeing successful acquisitions.

As you will discover, the true function of an acquisition is not just growth but recalibration. Buying another company will change yours for better or worse, depending on how strategically you approach the deal. By the same token, M&A activity as a whole serves to recalibrate entire industries. It is one of the market's most effective mechanisms for self-correction and positive evolution.

The better you understand acquisitions, the better you understand business itself.

FROM BEGINNING TO BEGINNING

I want to completely change how you see M&A. Experience has convinced me that the field is radically misunderstood by most people outside of it and by an alarming number of those who actually manage acquisitions. That 77 percent failure rate has nothing to do with luck. It is the telltale statistic of widespread ignorance.

I often encounter clients who tell me, "Yes, we have an in-house M&A expert. . . ." It turns out the expert really does know a lot—about due diligence, or company valuation, or negotiation. The problem is that a chef who has mastered only pastries is unlikely to run a profitable restaurant.

Buying a company successfully depends on knowing more than one piece well. It requires your mastery of an entire integrated process, with all the functions working together. I cannot emphasize this distinction too strongly. There is one theme underlying every chapter of this book: A successful acquisition must be 100 percent strategic in concept, planning, and execution. If these things are done right, even financially driven acquisitions that seem to be fast and opportunistic will be based on an underlying strategy. From the outside, these high-speed transactions can look deceptively casual, but the skilled operator is always making criteria-driven decisions and knows exactly when to say "yes" or "no."

The principle I am underlining here sounds self-evident, yet it is amazing how many impulse purchases occur in the mid-market sector. Someone sees an opportunity, gets excited about it, invents a plethora of reasons to buy, and launches into unplanned negotiations. The costs are huge: In fact, it has been calculated that most acquisitions end in failure of one kind or another. Sensing this, too many mid-market companies are scared off acquisition as a dangerous path to take. Without a plan, it is indeed a dangerous path. But with the detailed roadmap I will give you, buying another company can prove the fastest, most secure, and most profitable way to grow your own.

When I am teaching M&A, I often use the phrase "from beginning to beginning." I am signaling a difference from the more familiar phrase "from beginning to end," which suggests that once the deal is signed, the process is over. In my experience, the end of an M&A transaction marks the beginning of a whole new business reality, the merged entity. Between those two beginnings lies a sequence of fourteen steps, each of which must be diligently completed. At my firm, we call these steps "the Roadmap to Acquisitions."

I have the privilege of leading a team of consultants and analysts who are all fully aligned with the Roadmap approach. It's a system that's been developed, tested, and refined through some two decades of service to growing companies. We have learned the hard way what works and what doesn't. In the pages that follow, I share the fruits of our collective experience and guide you through each of the steps as thoroughly as this short book allows.

You will see that there is more involved in M&A than valuation formulae or negotiating tactics. You will discover how significant the human factor is, as the story of George and Anthony illustrates. You will grasp the difference between valuation and price, and between price and what I call "the seller's equation." You will realize that negotiation is a different game when you plan to work with your counterpart for years to come after the transaction is complete. You will find that the problems with integration that beset so many deals usually have their roots right at the beginning of the process. You will also learn how to select and use expert advisers—and how to keep them in their place.

This book is written for CEOs like George and for his counterparts in the corporate world who are looking for growth through acquisitions. It is for company executives and the people who advise them. It is also for mid-level managers charged with strategizing growth, to help them do a better job and advance their own professional expertise. My practice has tended to center on privately owned companies, and that is reflected in the stories you will find here. However, executives of publicly traded companies will find that the principles outlined here apply equally to the corporate mega-deal. Most of all, this book is for everyone interested in the business of business, because mastering the art of acquisitions requires us to grasp the complex dynamics of a living company.

There is a lot of information packed between these covers. My overriding wish, though, is to make M&A more accessible to more participants and to expand your horizons on the subject of company acquisitions.

THE HIDDEN OPPORTUNITY

The right acquisition can dramatically accelerate your company's growth. Sadly, the opportunities are widely missed, especially in the mid-market. There are many companies that would benefit from an external growth program, yet they shy away because the whole field of M&A seems too intimidating. There are other companies that attempt acquisitions and are disappointed by the outcome, largely because they have tried to follow a rote system overly focused on the numbers. I hope to demonstrate to you just how valuable the benefits of acquisition can be if you take an approach that is thoroughly disciplined on the one hand, and sufficiently holistic on the other.

When I say "holistic," I mean you have to go beyond the numbers. Of course, you are in business to make a profit, and you will approach an acquisition with every intention to make more money. The finances are an essential dimension of the M&A picture, but they are only one dimension. For success in this field, you must open your eyes to many other considerations.

Let's look, first of all, at the value that a successful acquisition might bring to your business. Many CEOs rush to buy with one objective only: to cut costs. This can be a legitimate motive and probably involves buying a competitor to consolidate your operations. But cutting costs is by no means the only reason to make an acquisition. There can be many others that deliver equal or greater value to your company. We will review these in detail later, but let me enumerate a few of them here.

Your acquisition might bring you a technology that you couldn't otherwise obtain. It could take you to a market sector that has been out of reach. It might win you exceptionally talented people. It could subtly but significantly enhance your brand and reputation, making you more attractive to customers and high-value employees. Or your acquisition could be simply defensive, blocking a competitor from obtaining the same assets.

While these benefits may represent values that are not subject to instant financial calculation, each of them can impact the bottom line in the long term.

Often, the single most important benefit of a judicious acquisition can be to "recalibrate" your business. (I explain this in detail later on.) In the simplest terms, what I mean is that every healthy business has to redefine itself over and over again to flourish in a changing world. Acquisitions—and divestitures—can be a swift and powerful way to positively reinvent your company to meet new pressures and leverage new opportunities.

There is one caveat, though. The good that can come from an external growth strategy may require you to revise, or even reverse, your assumptions about how to make an acquisition. There is an old way and a new way to go about the M&A process. It's important to recognize the difference.

THE OLD WAY AND THE NEW WAY

My firm had a client in the health services industry that perfectly exemplified the old way of approaching acquisitions. Judy, the

CEO, would be regularly approached by investment bankers hawking "the book" on a company they had for sale. She would listen to the pitch, peruse the documentation, and try to figure out whether the purchase was a good idea. Being committed to growth, she did her best to stay open to all the opportunities that were thrown at her, and eventually she allowed herself to be sold on acquiring a manufacturer of nurses' uniforms. The target company was losing money, but she was persuaded that she could easily turn it around and generate a profit. Twelve months later, the acquisition had become a disaster. Judy's troubles included an inherited lawsuit with an angry distributor, a serious absence of sales aggressiveness, and an unexpected trade restriction that slowed uniform production. She was not only losing money but also suffering a series of headaches that distracted her management team from their core business.

What was missing for Judy can be summed up in one word: strategy. And what I find remarkable is how common this problem is. Many quite sophisticated business leaders allow themselves to drift into a purely reactive relationship to growth. They listen to whoever comes to lunch, size up whatever opportunity comes across their desk, and get caught in the lure of the deal.

We insisted that Judy immediately adopt a strategic approach. She and her team worked intensely to learn the Roadmap methodology for a successful acquisition program (which you will read about in this book). We began with a Growth Program Review, as we always do, which creates the game plan in a highly structured manner. In the Growth Program Review for Judy's company, we established a team that reviewed the growth options in the light of the CEO's overall strategic vision, and then identified highly specific criteria for an acquisition

Most important, we shifted from a reactive to a proactive stance. Attention turned from the for-sale companies hawked around by investment bankers to not-for-sale companies that we had to seek out. I explained to Judy that every company is for sale—for the right equation. At the same time, we created an action plan to divest the new money-losing division. Today, Judy's health services company is growing apace and profitably so. Judy has discovered the tangible and intangible benefits of successful acquisition and learned a process that she can repeat in the years to come.

IT'S NOT A USED CAR

A very different client made my efforts to support his growth impossible. He was a successful CEO in the textile industry, a sector increasingly pressured by globalization. My client had a good understanding of the philosophy I am sharing with you here. Unfortunately, he over-delegated the acquisition process to his CFO. Like many (but not all) financial people, this character could see only the spreadsheets. He had zero patience for the "soft" side of acquisition deals—the management of emotions and relationships, which turns out not to be so soft when it sabotages the transaction.

For our hard-nosed CFO, everything was about beating down the other side to get the lowest possible price. There is one situation where this approach is legitimate—when you plan to close your acquisition and sell the assets. More often than not, however, you are seeking to buy a going concern that you intend to nourish and expand after the purchase. This means that after the acquisition is consummated, you will still be dealing with the people who face you around the negotiating table. When integration begins, they will remember how you treated them, and you will pay for your miscalculations—very likely in hard dollars. Buying a company is not like buying a car, where you walk away and never see the seller again. In many cases, it is more like buying an automobile with the seller thrown in. Imagine yourself at a dealership where you have to take the salesperson home with the car. You would probably negotiate a little differently!

The refusal to accommodate the human dimension is the root cause of many, if not most, M&A failures. Obsessive focus on negotiated wins and financial engineering can deliver you a Pyrrhic victory. You get what you ask for, but not what you need. Conversely, your ability to take a dimensional approach can put you way ahead of the game and enable you to achieve results over the heads of buyers with more cash in their hands.

To be clear here, I am all in favor of vigorous negotiation and taking a stand for your financial goals. However, successful acquisition also demands a breadth of business awareness and an informed understanding of the many dimensions of M&A.

THE SELLER'S EQUATION

In later chapters, I will discuss the concept of the *seller's equation*. It is such a key idea, though, that I introduce it here so you can bear it in mind right from the start. The seller's equation refers to the configuration of benefits, which usually goes beyond price, for which an owner will let go of his or her company.

I recall a client, Michael, who ran a highly successful wealth management company with several affiliate offices in three southwestern states. After we conducted our Growth Program Review with Michael, he decided to buy a similar company in the northwest. We looked at many candidates and settled on one business in particular that seemed a good fit, both financially and philosophically. That company's CEO, Terry, had an outlook on the business that resonated perfectly with Michael's. We knew that the success of the target company was largely due to Terry's vision and leadership, but we accepted that he would likely want to move on once he had collected the sizeable payment we were offering. How wrong we turned out to be.

As always, we focused the negotiations on our vision for the future rather than the price of the deal. Terry was inspired by Michael's plans. He committed to stay for at least a year at the helm of the northwest division and was given a seat on the board of the new entity. Four years later, he was still there, and I asked him why.

"Before, I was running a company. Now, I'm running a business," he replied. Like so many founder-entrepreneurs, when Terry had owned the company, he had suffered the frustrations of everyday firefighting—worrying about the computers, the payroll, health insurance, and repairs to the building. In his new role, he was freed from all this. The acquisition allowed him to be repositioned as a true strategist, which was the passion that had brought him into business in the first place. Of course, there was great personal satisfaction in this outcome. Just as significant were the consistent, profitable results he brought to the newly merged entity. All of this was possible only because we took the trouble to figure out Terry's personal seller's equation.

SYSTEM BREEDS SUCCESS

The emphasis I have given to the human dimension of the acquisition separates this book from others you might read about M&A. Let me balance that with an equal and opposite emphasis on system. The reactive character of the "old way" means that M&A transactions are often alarmingly haphazard. One specific reason is that the process involves several different experts who traditionally show up at different stages along the road, like cameo performers in a soap opera. This is a recipe for fragmentation.

I believe passionately in a highly structured and disciplined approach to acquisition, always beginning with a Growth Program Review. There are steps to take in the right way and in the right sequence. If you skip any one of them—and many buyers do—you are likely to fail, either by not completing the transaction or by triggering a chaotic integration.

When I explain this to clients, I often use the analogy of hiring employees. It's striking to note that most companies of any size have an exhaustive written process for hiring, with steps for attracting, interviewing, vetting, and selecting candidates. Yet even the most prized employee represents a modest risk. You pay for your investment incrementally, you are likely to get value back in a few months, and you can usually reverse your decision at any time. Buying a company involves a much larger investment and carries far greater risks if it goes wrong. You must commit massive resources for a return that may not appear for several years. So let me ask you this: Does your company have a written procedures manual for buying companies? Almost certainly not. My purpose in *Successful Acquisitions* is to help you fill that gap.

The Roadmap to Acquisitions (see Figure I-1) breaks into three main phases, which I define as:

1. Build the Foundations
2. Build the Relationships
3. Build the Deal

The Roadmap to Acquisitions

Figure I-1. An overview of the Roadmap approach.

The first phase, *Build the Foundations*, is more about you than about your acquisition. This is where you take your bearings, conduct a reality check on your current business situation, and establish a viable strategy for growth. The second phase, *Build the Relationships*, is courtship: researching prospective partners, making initial overtures, and developing a dialogue of trust. In the third phase, *Build the Deal*, you get down to the nitty-gritty of due diligence, deal structure, closing the transaction, and integrating the entities. Most players in the M&A game skip over the first phase, rush through the second, and get bogged down in the third. My approach pays thorough and skilled attention to the first two phases to ensure a swift and relatively trouble-free journey through the third.

The principle guiding all of this is your commitment to strategy. There are enough uncontrollable variables in life without abandoning ourselves to a reactive growth path. Decide who you are, where you want to be, and how you are going to get there. If serendipity throws an opportunity at your feet, especially as a pitch for a company someone is eager to sell, treat it with utmost caution. If that opportunity precisely matches the criteria that you have already defined, follow it up. If it does not, move on. When it comes to external growth, you—not chance—must be the master of your destiny.

My intention is to place in your hands a user's manual for buying companies. To support this, the book includes charts and simple tools to get you started on an active process. The single most important tool is the one-page Roadmap (shown in Figure I-1) that lays out each of the steps for the three main stages: *Build the Foundations, Build the Relationships,* and *Build the Deal*. Other tools include blueprints for establishing both market and company criteria—a crucial step in the planning process. There are also detailed equations for calculating the financial aspects of valuation.

You'll have noticed that when consultants publish a book, many of them reveal just a part of their recipe, in hopes that readers will turn to them for the missing ingredients. With *Successful Acquisi-*

tions, I made the decision to hold nothing back. Every step of the acquisition process I use in my practice is laid out for all to see. In the course of the book, I do explain the role and value of third-party advisers, but these pages contain all the information you need to conduct the entire acquisition process alone.

My hope is that you will achieve a positive result from the information I am sharing, just as my clients have done. Please let me know how you fare and if you have any questions arising from the book. As time and resources allow, I will do my best to respond to your communications.

You can reach me at David@SuccessfulAcquisitions.net.

All success on the road to growth!

❖ ❖ ❖

A note about the stories: The stories I share with you are true in essence, and most are drawn directly from my consulting experience as CEO of an M&A consulting firm. But as you will understand, I have changed some details—often including the industry—to protect my clients' anonymity.

PART 1

BUILD THE FOUNDATIONS

CHAPTER 1

KNOW THYSELF

MY ASSUMPTION IN THIS BOOK IS that you are ambitious for growth and are seriously considering acquisition as a way to reach your goals. So here we are together, embarking on a journey that will demand a great deal of learning, persistence, discipline, and flexibility. The purpose of this chapter is to prepare you adequately for the challenges ahead.

Because growth, especially external growth, turns our attention to opportunities in the world beyond our own operation, it's easy to rush into action without an adequate review of where we are coming from. This would be a big mistake, so the first and essential step in the Roadmap to Acquisitions process is to look within. Before you grow your company, you need to develop the best possible understanding of it. By "best," I mean the most accurate, the most dimensional, and the most practical. This is obvious if you think about it. The outcome of your growth program may be a marriage of some kind, and you will be scrutinizing many potential partners. But how do you judge if the match is good without understanding yourself as well as you do the acquisition target?

As a CEO or senior executive, you may feel that you know

everything about your company that can be known, especially if you are the founder. In reality, my consulting experience tells me otherwise. Over time, owners get consumed in the effort to hold things together and keep their enterprise on the road. Their original vision gets obscured by the dust they kick up as they drive along. It takes a strong intention to pull away from day-to-day issues and review your company as an organic whole.

The discipline of introspection has a double benefit. Not only does it provide a rational foundation for making growth decisions, but it also gives you practice in the kind of analysis you will apply to potential acquisitions. "Know thyself" is the prerequisite to knowing others, on a company level as well as for individuals. Ignorance of self, conversely, dims your eyesight. It renders you less perceptive when you come to assess prospective partners in growth. Not surprisingly, true self-knowledge is as rare on the corporate level as it is among individuals. It takes the kind of effort and attention that your daily business activities simply do not usually require.

So in this process, I will be taking you through the kind of self-exploration that I teach my clients. If you are the owner, I would expect you to experience a mixture of confirmation and surprise, of meeting the all-too-familiar and spotting a few things that perhaps you knew but never really wanted to know. If you are a senior employee, I advise you to find a tactful way to engage the owner in the process. When my firm works with clients, we function as a team involving all the people who are likely to play a key role in future external growth activities.

THE SEVEN STRATEGIC QUESTIONS

In any business endeavor, having the right questions is often half the battle. For this review, we will work with seven powerful questions that I have tried and tested with dozens of clients at the outset of their growth program. Here are the seven questions you will need to answer:

1. What business are we in?
2. What is our core competency?
3. What are we not?
4. Where is our pain?
5. What are our dreams?
6. What is our risk tolerance?
7. What is our company DNA?

In the coming pages, I will explore each question with you in some detail. You will gain the most benefit if you break off from reading at each step and make some brief written notes of your insights and observations. (If it helps, you can use the self-assessment tool in Figure 1-2 at the end of this chapter.) At each stage, I point out how the question we are addressing impacts growth strategy. This is important to bear in mind. We are not conducting a theoretical exercise in navel-gazing. The information you produce will be decisive as you venture out in search of acquisition partners.

"What Business Are We In?"

Let's admit it right away: This is a trick question. The correct answer is usually not the first answer. Here's a classic example from the annals of corporate America: Union Pacific thought they were in the business of railroads—the commonsense answer. In reality, they were in the business of mass transportation. Had they recognized this early enough, they might today be flying planes or building hybrid cars. Here's a more recent example. A client of ours supplying the upper end of the bicycle industry thought they were in the business of making brake mechanisms. Their special capacity was in lightweight solutions, and we resolved that they were in fact in the business of making racing bikes faster. This realization led to a strategic expansion into gear systems. It took a process of careful self-examination to discover what now looks obvious but was not when we began.

So exactly what business are *you* in? Among all the mass of activity your company is engaged in, where is the beating heart? Step back, look at the big picture, and ask yourself: "What is our business really about?" The answer should be as short as you can make it:

- "We are in the custom car auto parts business."
- "We are in the investment advice business."
- "We are in the residential community planning business."
- "We are in the organic fertilizer business."

You may need to take several shots at this. There is a tendency to either be too granular ("railroads" rather than "transportation") or too global ("creating exceptional customer satisfaction"). Remember that growth is your purpose. You need to define your business in a way that sets a trajectory broad enough for expansion and focused enough to stay on track.

Getting a clear answer to this first strategic question may, in fact, require you to address the other six. So I suggest you make an initial attempt at it now, and then return to review and possibly revise your answer when you have considered the other questions.

The challenge of knowing what business you are in goes beyond how you define your product or service. It extends to the kind of customers you are seeking. Here is one question I have found especially revealing: "Assuming the same revenue outcome, would you rather have 10,000 low-value customers or 1,000 high-value customers?"

Take a moment to answer this candidly. If you are inclined to take the 10,000, you are more likely to be at the commodity end of the market. Nothing wrong with that, although it definitely carries challenges. That choice may also indicate you have more confidence in your marketing than in your product (a distinction we explore in the next segment on core competencies). If you prefer the 1,000 high-value customers, that suggests to me that you have the potential for a strongly branded position, and you probably see unique strengths in your product or service. To flourish at this end of the spectrum, you should also have considerable confidence in your capacity for customer retention. In that case, you are a relationship company.

So what business *are* you in? Don't underestimate how powerful this apparently simple question can be. Your decision will almost certainly impact the trajectory of growth you choose. What makes this so important is that in a world of rapid change and expanding global markets, you face an almost intolerable surfeit of opportunities. Without being anchored in a strong, unmistakable self-definition, you will be easily dragged this way and that.

"What Is Our Core Competency?"

Sometimes history is powerful. We once had a client who thought he was in the business of manufacturing pet toys. He was consumed with questions of how to extend his product lines and enhance his production technologies. Once we drilled down with the question of core competencies, we discovered he was really a peddler—and a very good one, too. The client's founder, long since passed away, was a brilliant salesman who had gradually taken control of the manufacturing company he'd worked for in the last phase of his life. His son, the current owner and our client, had assumed not only his father's mantle but also his magical knack for sales. So we built a growth plan around this discovery, bringing him back to his roots and strengths.

Your company's core competency may well be influenced by its history. It may be reflected in the kind of hiring decisions you make and where the greatest talents lie. How your market perceives you can also tell you a lot, as does where you are making the most money.

The point is that companies, like people, often have mistaken ideas about where they truly excel. And like people, they sometimes need an outsider to shake off their illusions and get clear about the reality. So when you go in search of your core competency, follow some simple guidelines:

- Don't trust your own assumptions.
- Look at your company from functional angles.
- See where your resources are concentrated.
- See where your successes are concentrated.
- Ask informed and intelligent outsiders.

Here are some specific tactics that can help you focus on your core competency. Review the key functions of your company—operations, marketing, sales, finance, management—and ask yourself which is the strongest and which is the weakest. If you have a superb manufacturing plant staffed by the best in the business, but your sales team is struggling and your marketing strategy is gathering dust, it's pretty obvious where your strength lies.

Another tactic is to view your company in a competitive context. What do you do differently and better than your nearest competitors? What do clients seek you out for? Why do they stay? Is it something about the product itself or a quality of your service and how you deliver? Or is it a perceived value in your brand, a matter of historic reputation, or newcomer's cool?

If you see your strength in technology or product, take a close look to see if you have the *best* technology or the *winning* technology. There is a significant difference between "best" and "winning," as those who remember the sad story of Beta and VHS well know. While Beta remained the trade standard for videocassette tapes, VHS owned the huge consumer space prior to DVD. The best technology wins awards, rave reviews, and an honored place in the Smithsonian. The winning technology is the one that does the job and is coupled with an effective marketing strategy that installs it as the solution of choice.

Other ways to identify your strengths are to look at your employee retention. If turnover is high, what weakness does this reveal and where is the compensating strength? If employees tend to stay with you for the long haul, why? (If you don't know, ask them!)

Perhaps your strength lies in a culture of innovation. To be objective about this, you can review your investment in R&D relative to industry norms, the number of patents you hold, and the kind of encouragement you give employees to generate new ideas.

Some companies are masters at neither technology nor marketing per se, but they have an exceptional capacity in distribution. They can move product quickly and effectively to all corners of the earth and show up on the shelves of the least expected outlets. Is this you? Or is distribution something of an Achilles' heel?

Knowing your core competency and the associated strengths is a truly critical factor in building your growth strategy. For one thing, you will be looking to leverage those strengths as you expand, rather than taking them for granted. Then you will seek to complement them by finding external resources that compensate for your weaknesses. Finally, your strengths represent a marketing asset when you approach a potential acquisition. As you will discover, the strategic buyer actually has to sell himself. Your strengths are part of the story that will make a seller take interest in a potential union.

"What Are We Not?"

This is really a subset of questions one and two, but it is so powerful it deserves separate attention. (For companies with a single product or highly focused offering, the question "What are we not?" poses no difficulty and you can quickly move on.)

As an enterprise expands and becomes more complex, this issue becomes one of crucial strategic importance. Rapid success often blinds owners and leads them into areas where they have no business to be.

When you answer this question, you needn't list all the obvious things you are not. If you are a dental technology company, of course you are not a mortgage broker. The point is to list the possibilities you might be kidding yourself about. This takes some attention to subtleties. For example, you are a dental technology company, not a general medical technology company. Or you are a dental technology design company, not a dental technology manufacturer. It is those areas that legitimately lie on the margin of your operations that can confuse the picture.

Needless to say, just because you are not something today doesn't mean you cannot become it tomorrow. The important thing is that any move from what you are to what you can be should be conscious and intentional, and not based on a misconception of your starting point.

Here's why. By blurring the boundary between what you are and what you are not, you can deceive yourself about competencies. I had a client that made fish products for manufacturers, which in turn created packaged delicacies for the end consumer. My client was tempted at one stage to drift into making consumer products themselves, but they had absolutely no experience or competency in this area. It seemed to them that it was just a step away, but actually, there was a gulf between the two competencies.

So this is what to do when you review the question "What are we not?" Look at what business you are in and where your core competencies are. Identify the closest cousins that surround those core essentials. Make a list of the business activities and sectors closest to your own. You are now staring at a list of pitfalls—pitfalls that *could* become opportunities, but only if you proceed with eyes wide open.

"Where Is Our Pain?"

For most companies, this is usually an easy question to answer—
painfully easy! My assumption is that your pain involves some kind
of barrier to growth. What stands in the way of your reaching that
next, elusive level?

The barriers you face probably lie in one of the key functional
areas that exist in every business:

- **Operations:** The creation of your product or service
- **Marketing:** How your product is getting to customers
- **Finance:** Your capacity to implement the decisions you make
- **Management and personnel:** Your human capital

We can break these down easily enough. If your operations are
problematic, it could be because of a systems deficiency, inadequate
technology, or a gap in human resources. If your marketing is weak,
internal reasons might include lack of brand strategy (very common
and underdiagnosed), a weakness of message, lack of targeting, or
insufficient resources. External reasons could be changes in demand
or new competition. Regarding finance, internal issues can include
cash flow constrictions or debt problems, while external pressures
may come from factors such as interest rates. As for management
and personnel, you might be lacking in a specialty expertise or in
the capacity to drive performance required for aggressive growth.
There can be a host of other problems not listed here. The likelihood
is that you know what they are.

Or do you?

In chiropractic medicine, there is a telling concept called
"referred pain." Your foot hurts and you go to the podiatrist, but it
still doesn't get better. How so? It transpires that your foot pain
may originate from a misaligned vertebra. The pain shows up in a
location that is different from where the problem originated. In

business terms, your failure to attract a key human resource may reflect a branding problem. Marketing may be getting dragged down by operations. Cash flow anxieties might be best relieved by over-hauling the sales process.

In other words, when we use a functional model to diagnose business problems, we need both an analytic and a holistic approach. This has immediate bearings on growth strategy, because insofar as your growth plans are influenced by your current pain, you want to be sure you are curing the disease, not just masking the symptom.

For example, when revenues flatten, it is easy to conclude that what is needed is simply a greater number of customers. You could launch into an acquisition program based on that assumption, failing to recognize that your real problem is customer retention. You buy a company that gives you thousands of new customers, and you start losing those, too. Perhaps the partner you need is one with outstanding service methodologies and a great CRM system—not just more customers.

Correctly identifying your company pain, like diagnosing a physical malady, may best be done with the help of an outside expert who has no history, no agenda, and no investment one way or the other in a particular solution.

"What Are Our Dreams?"

On the wall of my company office there is a large inscription:

> # WE HELP CLIENTS IMPLEMENT THEIR DREAMS

Note that the inscription refers to dreams, not goals. There is a difference. Goals are essential, the very stuff of successful business growth. But goals are the junior partners of something bigger.

When Bill Gates founded Microsoft, he had a dream of seeing a

PC on every desk. This was in the antediluvian epoch of massive mainframes occupying thousands of square feet. You couldn't call Gates's dream a goal. It was too remote and unreasonable. Rather, it was a creative vision, an idea of the possible. It saturated his company and shaped its DNA, while he was busy meeting goals like raising finance and making a deal with IBM. Though it has effectively been fulfilled, the spirit of that founding idea still characterizes the Microsoft ethos. It is part of what makes Microsoft the global master it is today.

I encourage you to plan your external growth in relation to your dreams, not just your goals. The reason is that an acquisition impacts your company's core, its essential personality, like almost nothing else. If you focus too much on immediate goals, like hitting a certain revenue level or capturing a targeted market share, you risk betraying that original dream. The price to pay for that can be devastating in terms of problematic integration or a completely failed acquisition.

If you do attend to what I call the "company dream," you may turn down an acquisition opportunity that makes total sense on the spreadsheets but clashes with a higher-level value. If your dream includes setting a new standard for personal service in your industry, then buying a company whose entire culture is inimical to good service could be a mistake even if it would expand your customer base.

In my experience, few company owners are exclusively motivated by money. Most have a vision of something they want to contribute to their industry or to the world at large. This may be very specific, like an exciting advance in production efficiencies, or it may be broad, like a new model of how to help clients solve problems. As the Microsoft example illustrates, these big-picture ambitions are not a peripheral luxury. They permeate the company from top to bottom.

So how do you identify what I am calling the company dream? It's really about going upstream, looking at your goals, and asking:

Why is this important? Eventually, as you ask that question repeatedly, you arrive at the founding values of your enterprise, its reason for existence.

There is a secondary benefit to this approach. By researching your own company dream, you train yourself to be alert to the dream that drives a potential target. This can be enormously important, as you will see when we explore seller psychology in Chapters 7 and 8. You may well be able to acquire a company for less than a competing buyer because you demonstrate a clearer understanding of why the owners are in business. I know because I have done just that for several clients.

"What Is Our Risk Tolerance?"

You cannot advance a growth strategy that pushes too far beyond the level of risk that is acceptable to your company. This is first and foremost a question of the shareholders' tolerance, for they are the people who ultimately bear the consequences if things go wrong. If you are the sole owner, the level of risk tolerance is fairly easy to establish. If there are multiple owners, as is often the case, then answering the question is a little harder.

As a consultant, I ask people about their risk tolerance directly, and this yields a certain amount of useful information. Perhaps more valuable, though, is looking at what they actually do. We often misjudge our own relation to risk and imagine our tolerance is lower or higher than it actually is.

Here are two simple ways to discover your company's risk tolerance level. First, look at the balance sheet. If the company is cash-rich and debt-free, that tells you the tolerance for risk is probably very low—more common than not for privately held companies. If, on the other hand, there is a significant debt-to-equity ratio, you have an enterprise that is willing to exploit the benefits of leverage and assume the inevitable risks that come with debt.

The second way to reveal risk tolerance is to study your process for buying capital equipment. If the process is fairly swift and is delegated to relatively few individuals, risk tolerance is probably quite high. If the process is laborious, with complex approval procedures involving many people, risk tolerance is more likely low.

How does this impact growth strategy? Again, there are several ramifications. First, the kinds of growth tactics you select, and the financial models required, will be directly limited by the level of risk you are willing to assume. More than that, the kinds of partners you will feel comfortable with are likely to have a similar risk tolerance. Otherwise, you will face integration nightmares. If your shareholders have very low risk tolerance and you acquire a company that is highly leveraged and makes rapid spending decisions, there is likely to be a backwash of anxiety that will quickly reach your boardroom. Conversely, if your owners are fairly adventurous and you buy a company that is extremely risk-averse, you will face constant headaches trying to move the new partner into action.

"What Is Our Company DNA?"

By DNA, I mean the overall character of your company, in the sense that one talks about an individual's character. Certainly, this is defined by your corporate values and the company dream we have just spoken of. Beware, though. The company DNA cannot be read off a nicely worded mission statement hanging in your reception area. It is most vividly expressed by what actually happens, day by day, inside the four walls of your company.

People often speak in this respect of "corporate culture," but that phrase is too restrictive. It suggests dress codes or the time employees clock in. These are actually significant indicators, but what constitutes your company DNA goes far wider and deeper (see Figure 1-1).

As in the human body, your DNA is the aspect of the company that is least likely to change. Financials rise and fall. Employees come and go. IT systems can be replaced. Procedures get rewritten,

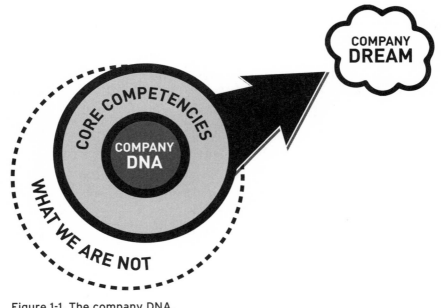

Figure 1-1. The company DNA.

product lines are added or removed, and marketing strategies get turned upside down. All these are important, but transient, realities of business life. However, there is something about your company that remains stubbornly the same throughout the vicissitudes of the business environment—in other words, its DNA.

Here are some key questions to unveil this permanent strand:

- How are decisions made? By top-down command, or collaboratively? Slowly and ruminatively, or rapidly and instinctively?
- How are hiring choices arrived at? Strictly on credentials and capabilities, or just as much on personality and team fit?
- What level of autonomy is given to departments and individuals?
- How focused is the company on innovation?

- What value is really placed on customer service?
- Is the company more strategically driven, or more opportunistic and reactive?
- What is the attitude to pricing and discounts?
- How aggressively do you tend to pursue new business, new technologies, or new talent?

The process of investigating your company DNA has at least two key consequences for your growth strategy. It helps you identify which avenues of growth are most likely to fit the mold and which potential acquisition targets would make good collaborators. It also gives you tremendous practice in sizing up those targets. Just as you need to know your own DNA, you want to know your future partner's. Both of you need to take a blood test before any marriage is considered.

CAUTIONARY TALES

Few entrepreneurs I know are introspective by nature, and this exercise in self-examination may be a little hard to take if you are impatient to get immediately into action. To underline just how important is the injunction "Know thyself," let me point to two very different examples, one in my own experience dealing with mid-market companies and one in the public domain.

My firm had a client in the medical technology field that wanted to grow. There were twelve people on the management team we worked with, all with passionate views on what their company was about and where it should go next. The company's focus was highly specialized optical components for surgical instruments that look inside the body.

In terms of growth, these twelve strong-willed characters fell into three camps. One camp wanted to grow the company by expanding outside the medical field, selling specialist optical components to the defense industry in particular. Another wanted to branch into other aspects of medical technologies, such as advanced scanners and EEG machines. The third camp wanted to stay in the medical market but get out of manufacturing altogether, and instead leverage their expertise through consulting services and equipment service and maintenance.

Now, on one level, this represents a classic example of the kinds of choices every company faces when it seeks growth. (We will review this in more detail in Chapter 2, when we look at the Michael Porter model of Five Forces analysis.) The point of my story is that after three months of wrangling, our client was completely unable to make a decision. A year later, as I write this, they have still not made an acquisition, and their external growth program is effectively stalled.

Here is the root of the problem. The management team couldn't agree on a plan for growth because they couldn't agree on who they are now. There was no consensus on what business they were in. There was no consensus on what their core competencies were. There was no consensus on where their pain lay. One group was saying, "We are optical specialists"; another was saying, "We are a medical technology company"; and the third was saying, "We are really a consulting firm." Each group had a different view of the present, and that inevitably translated into radically different visions for the future.

As for the example from the public domain, this chapter would not be complete without a reference to the debacle of the AOL–Time Warner merger of 2001, which will forever remain a landmark in U.S. business history. Obviously, there were many complex factors that led to this sorry disaster. On a very simple level, both sides failed to look *inside* before they launched into a courtship. A major problem, as everyone now knows, is that the two companies had radically different DNA. Time Warner was a traditional command-and-control, risk-averse corporation of the old school. AOL was one of the first in a new generation of tech-savvy, venturesome,

	TODAY	5 YEARS	10 YEARS
SHAREHOLDERS			
EXECUTIVES			
MANAGERS			
EMPLOYEES			

Figure 1-2. A simple company self-assessment tool.

informal, collaborative companies that have been birthed by the Internet. My suspicion is that the parties to this deal were one-dimensional in their analysis. They were probably over-seduced by the lure of a massive exercise in financial engineering. This is a common trap for publicly traded companies driven to deliver quarterly value to their shareholders. In the process, people gloss over the apparently peripheral issue of the company DNA. In fact, though, this factor is far from peripheral. It can literally make or break the outcome of the deal.

In the next chapter, we begin work on your growth strategy itself. Before we go there, I implore you to step back, take a fresh look at your company, and ask: "Who exactly are we? And what do we want to be when we grow up?" To start the process, use the simple but effective self-assessment tool in Figure 1-2. Where does each group listed see your company today? Where does each group see your company in five and ten years?

CHAPTER 2

PATHWAYS TO GROWTH

YOU KNOW THE MAXIM: *Grow or die.* Growth is in the very nature of business. Once a company loses its appetite for expansion, it is almost certainly settling into decline. So now that you have looked inside your company and taken stock of where you stand today, it's time to look outward and forward. It is time for growth.

Our question here is not whether to grow, but how. In this chapter, you will discover that you are richer in choices than you probably realized. We explore five essential pathways, culminating in external growth. Then we review no less than nine forms of external growth. You will learn about the pros and cons of each option and how to select the tactic that best serves your objectives.

First, we must place the issue of growth in a strategic context. As a consultant approached by clients hungry to go out and buy something, I always insist that we begin with the 30,000-foot view and a rigorous Growth Program Review. This enables us to map the path forward in relation to the biggest picture of the business as it has been and is today.

GROWTH AS A TOOL FOR CALIBRATION

Common sense suggests that growth is simply about getting bigger: having more customers, more markets, more products, and more revenue. In reality, a successful growth strategy should enable you to become increasingly focused and effective. Certainly you are seeking an increase in profits, but higher earnings don't automatically flow from supersizing your company. In fact, the opposite can be true.

I prefer to see growth strategy as a way to *recalibrate* the company, bringing it into closer alignment with its inherent purpose and current market conditions. Recalibration is a continual necessity today, because economic and technological changes are remapping the business environment at such an extraordinary rate. We could rewrite the maxim we began with: *Recalibrate or die.*

What this means is that growth can sometimes mean doing *less* of something. It can mean shedding customers. It can even mean divesting whole divisions of your business. In my seminars on M&A, I often refer to the historic example of General Electric, an avaricious acquirer of other companies. I point out that for many years, GE tended to sell as many companies as it bought. A constant process of selling and buying enabled its management to define and redefine what this great corporation was really about.

Naturally, any idea of contraction is counterintuitive to the entrepreneurial owner whose eyes are fixed on a simple horizon of endless expansion. At my firm, when we introduce the recalibration concept to clients, we often meet initial resistance, but those who are willing to stay with the program see remarkable results.

Take, for example, a client of ours in the plastic molding business. They had several divisions, and they approached us because they were itching to buy another one. They weren't quite sure where to look, so we sat down with the owners and helped them conduct the "know thyself" process described in Chapter 1. One of their divisions made small product-wrapping machines, another produced the clasps for some high-end plastic food containers, yet another made a rather neat alternative to bubble wrap, and so forth. A brief word with the CFO revealed that no less than five of the six divisions were consistently losing money. No one had bothered too much about this because the core business was so profitable it kept the whole operation well above the waterline.

This was a privately owned business, with several family members who were active owners. It turned out that most of them treated the company as a kind of hobby, and the various divisions reflected their disarming amateur enthusiasm. We invited them to rethink their purpose before they took another step toward growth. After a few lengthy discussions, everyone became excited about the concept of recalibrating. We worked with them to design a program to divest all the loss-making divisions. At the same time, we analyzed their core business, plastic molding, to identify where the best opportunities for growth lay so that we could make plans for a targeted acquisition. In other words, growth here began with a dramatic *contraction*, saying good-bye to loyal customers and staff, letting go of technologies and markets, and taking a firm stand on what the company was not. From this reduced base, the company has expanded again. Today, the company is not as big as it was when I first became involved, but it is almost twice as profitable.

THE "FIVE FORCES" MODEL OF COMPANY GROWTH

When we begin work with clients on their Growth Program Review, we normally use Michael Porter's "Five Forces" model for analyzing a company's competitive position. It invites you to look at the pressures on your business from several key perspectives and provides a tool both for diagnosis and prescription (see Figure 2-1).

I like the Porter model because it pushes you to see beyond competition, where most business owners tend to get fixated. I recall a client in the financial software industry whose entire strategy consisted of a breathless reaction to what his competitors were doing. If they added a new function to their application, he set his team to

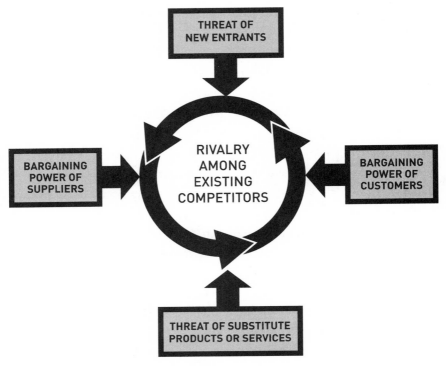

Figure 2-1. Michael Porter's "Five Forces" model.

work making a better version of the same upgrade. If his competitors broke into a new geographic market, he dispatched his sales team to set up office there. It was the ultimate "me-too-but-me-better" approach. Not a very robust recipe for growth.

The Five Forces model gets you asking a different set of questions, for example, how changes in supply might affect your business, or what barriers are faced by new entrants to the market, or where new technologies might displace your current offering. By far the most important element in Porter's model, to my mind, is "Customers," because this is the key to future demand. In fact, my one quarrel with the model is that Porter places this element to one side and leaves competitors and competition in the center. I usually reconfigure it to make "Customers"—that is, future demand—the centerpiece.

Possibly the single most important shift in thinking I introduce to my clients lies here. I pull their attention away from their competition and onto their market. Together, we break the spell of the present and lift our eyes to the future. Of course, future demand is always uncertain, unlike the current antics of our competition. As Henry R. Luce said, "Business, more than any other occupation, is a continual dealing with the future; it is a continual calculation, an instinctive exercise in foresight." Our task is to reduce uncertainty as far as we can by careful research and strategic analysis.

Future demand is king for reasons that are self-evident, once you pause to think about it. Ultimately, your growth depends on your success in meeting the needs of customers you have yet to capture. What do they want today? What *will* they want in the future? Business winners are the ones who best answer these two questions, especially the second. (You will see in later chapters how much painstaking effort we invest in market research and the lengths we go in our attempts to second-guess future trends.)

Once the orientation has shifted to future market demand, a tremendous clarity emerges in the strategic process. You have a basis for defining your criteria for decisions like which direction to grow, which growth tactics to adopt, where in the market to focus, and what to add to your current resources.

THE FIVE PATHWAYS TO GROWTH

As you focus your attention on the growth of your company, there are five key pathways to consider, as shown in Figure 2-2.

Although these choices are by no means equal in value, the important realization is that you do have a choice. I make my living mostly by helping clients buy companies. However, before we even start planning an acquisition, I take great care to place this tactic in

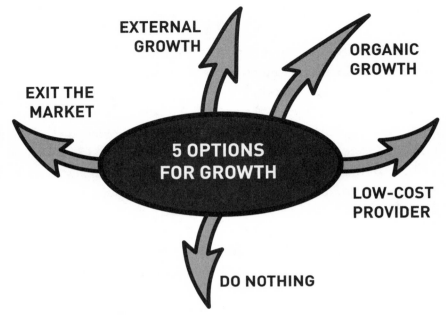

Figure 2-2. The five pathways to growth.

the broader context of growth options. That way, if and when my clients come to make a purchase, they know exactly why this path was chosen and not another.

So let's review the five pathways in more detail.

Grow Organically

Organic growth is business as usual. It is growth through acquiring more customers or selling more products. I assume you are reading this book because on some level your organic growth has stalled. But before you rush to adopt an alternative strategy, let's consider some of the creative ways companies can reenergize their organic growth.

I recall a company that went through the slow and painful discovery facing so many American manufacturers. My client's expertise was in small die-cast components, and they had a large collection of fairly old machines that churned out millions of these pieces every day for a variety of industrial customers. Not surprisingly, their customers were progressively defecting to cheaper sources in China and Southeast Asia. There was no way for my client to compete on price, so they undertook a serious self-examination. The solution here was to revisit the basics and for the owners to ask themselves who they were and what business they were really in. They knew they had exceptional expertise in their understanding of die-cast manufacture, but they had drifted into competing in commodity markets. They decided to refocus the company by providing highly specialized components to selected industries, especially aerospace. To pull this off, they needed to conduct a complete makeover. The founder traveled to Sweden to purchase the very latest technology. Meanwhile, he had his team clear out their plant, throw away all the junk, remodel the flooring, and repaint the whole building. By the time he had the new equipment installed, the plant looked like a microchip clean room. Now he was ready to invite his target prospects to visit and talk business. Within a year, the company had turned itself around. It became a valued source of extremely precise and hard-to-find components for a small segment of the aerospace industry. While the customer base shrunk tremendously, profits rose. This was organic growth through creative recalibration.

Another client provided galvanized steel, particularly for railings and protective barriers. One of their main competitors was concrete—a viable alternative for building barriers—which has one simple advantage. You can paint concrete, which makes for a wider choice of looks than the silver appearance produced by the zinc in galvanized steel. Again, this company needed to rethink who they were. They had become so identified with zinc that they neglected to realize they were in the business of providing solutions for railings and barriers. They made a simple adjustment and launched a new product line: paint for steel. Now they could add color to their product and provide a choice of looks to fend off the competition.

Here is one last example of inventive pathways to organic

growth. A company we worked with in the cabling business was struggling to differentiate themselves amid a rising tide of competitors. They realized that one product category in particular was proving challenging to install, and this was giving headaches to the architects and contractors responsible for figuring out how to wire new buildings. So my client created a certification program for this product line, training installers and providing them with a market seal of approval. The program had a double benefit: It was a revenue source in itself, as installers paid fees for the training and certifications. It also positioned my client as the effective industry leader in that product category.

The message in these stories is that a little imagination goes a long way. When organic growth stagnates, be prepared to go back to the fundamentals and review the questions we presented in Chapter 1. At the same time, be prepared to think outside the box and search for less-than-obvious solutions. You'll notice, incidentally, that each of the clients described above succeeded by paying close attention to changes in market demand. It is a theme we return to repeatedly.

Exit the Market

If your company's organic growth has hit a plateau or is in decline, leaving the current market is an option that should be seriously considered before you embark on any other growth solutions. With future demand as your guiding star, ask yourself if the odds are getting increasingly stacked against your success. Consider all the creative ways you can come up with to accelerate your organic growth, and if nothing pans out, take a long hard look at divestiture. Naturally, you want to match any shrinkage in one sector with a complementary plan for growth elsewhere. This will be dictated by your initial analysis of who you are and where your core competencies lie.

Sometimes the best pathway to growth is to get right out of the market you are in. I have already mentioned a couple of examples of companies that first contracted in order to grow. Here is another: In 2007, GE shed its $11.6 billion plastics division. This sector had become increasingly commoditized and therefore subject to aggressive foreign competition. It is also dangerously vulnerable to fluctuations in the price and supply of oil. For GE, the best way forward was to back out of plastics altogether and shift its energies toward other areas with growing future demand, for example, in the water industry.

Be the Low-Cost Provider

Sometimes, organic growth can be achieved by dramatically cutting costs. Again, growth in this case might appear more on the bottom line than in top-line revenues or size of market share. When I'm teaching, I call this "the jellyfish strategy": You go up when the tide rises and down when the tide recedes. There may not be many natural predators, so you survive, but this is clearly no way to drive long-term expansion.

Note that being the lowest cost provider is distinct from being the lowest priced. We have a client that makes quality dog food cheaper than any other player, but they sell it at market price. Their strength lies in their operations and technology, and all the benefit goes to their bottom line. In my experience, the lowest priced provider is rarely the lowest cost provider. That's because price-cutting tends to be the strategy of losers. Companies that resort to discounting rarely have the smarts to run a low-cost operation.

A very profitable company we once worked with made toothbrushes. They had one of the largest manufacturing plants I have seen in the privately held sector, thousands of square feet packed with machinery. It was run by six people. The company had made the effort—and taken the risks—of a massive investment in advanced technology to deliver product at a lower cost than most competitors. This proved a successful hedge against not only American but also offshore competition. Their pricing was low enough to hold their large brand-name clients. At the same time, their margins were significantly higher than the industry average.

Do Nothing

Of course, doing nothing is rarely if ever a pathway to growth. To do nothing is to drift with the tide, effectively letting your competitors set your course. I have to include it here, though, because it is a choice that companies actually make every day. "Choice" may be an overstatement. Few executives or board members sit down, open their flipcharts, and plan a careful do-nothing strategy. They drift into it by default. Inertia is one of the most powerful forces in the universe—and in business. When things seem to be going more or less satisfactorily, we all get tempted to keep doing what we are most accustomed to. However, the long-term costs can be disastrous.

Take a couple of well-known historic examples: Montgomery Ward and Kmart. These two retail giants both assumed that past success was a guarantee of future performance. But the world changed around them: Consumers became more demanding both for price and quality, while the supply chain was transformed by globalization. Now the companies are two great symbols of corporate failure. JCPenney came perilously close to the same fate, but it was rescued by an energetic management team determined to pull the company into the twenty-first century.

What does this mean for you? The main lesson is that the do-nothing strategy can creep up on you. One of my tasks at our firm is to make my clients nervous. Even when they are doing well, I need to keep them a little alarmed about what could happen next. Again, it comes down to a focus on future demand. No matter how healthy the market is today, where might it be heading tomorrow? Take a second look at your current business strategy and ask if you are assuming a future that is simply a repetition of the present. Then bombard your plans with a series of tough "what if?" questions. That is the outlook that separates a Walmart from a Kmart, or a Target from a Montgomery Ward.

Pursue External Growth

The fifth and final pathway we consider here is external growth. Here, expansion is achieved by engaging with entities outside the company itself. There are many forms of engagement, of which acquisition—the focus of this book—is but one. Though placed last on our list, external growth should not be seen as a last resort or the pathway to choose only if other courses are not available. In many cases, external growth should top your list of potential strategies. Our objective here is to ensure that you see external growth within the context of the other four alternatives. (See Figure 2-3 for a tool you can use to assess how the five pathways to growth would serve your company.)

	ATTEMPTED Y/N	PROS	CONS	CONSIDER Y/N
ORGANIC GROWTH				
EXIT THE MARKET				
LOW-COST PROVIDER				
DO NOTHING				
EXTERNAL GROWTH				

Figure 2-3. The growth checklist.

THE NINE PATHWAYS OF EXTERNAL GROWTH

We have explored some of the broad choices that are available to companies seeking growth. Now, it is time to look more deeply at the fifth and final pathway: external growth.

When it comes to external growth, buying another company is just one of *nine* possible tactics, and it may or may not be best for you. In the sections that follow, I invite you to consider the nine options in some detail. Again, my purpose is to ensure that if you choose to buy a company, it is in the context of all the possibilities for growth that lie before you:

1. Strategic alliance
2. Joint venture
3. Licensing
4. Toll manufacturing
5. Greenfielding
6. Franchising
7. Import/export
8. Minority interest
9. Acquisition

Strategic Alliance

Suppose you see the need to expand your customer base, but you have hit a ceiling with your current marketing and sales effort. One simple step you can take is to form an alliance with a partner who is serving the customers you seek with a noncompeting product. You can structure the arrangement in countless ways. Perhaps the partner benefits from simply being able to expand its offering; perhaps you pay a commission on sales or leads; or perhaps it is more of an exchange, whereby you simultaneously market your partner's product to your existing customer base.

The appeal, but also the risk, of such an arrangement lies in the absence of equity investment. Neither party has an ownership stake in the outcome. Of course, the legal contract of the alliance can have everything nailed down beautifully, but there is a significant difference, in terms of energy and commitment, between a legal obligation and a true business commitment.

The strategic alliance tends to the character of a one-night stand, and in fact, I advise our clients to restrict such alliances to short-term agreements. I also like to see alliances focused on very specific and limited objectives, such as securing a better network of representatives. With these caveats, the alliance tactic can deliver tangible benefits.

Nevertheless, the question is bound to arise at some point in the relationship: What next? If the alliance falters, the obvious outcome is to withdraw at the end of the contract. But what if it goes well? There may come a time when you try to figure how to get up to the next level, with some kind of equity involvement. I like to address this issue right from the beginning and write into the contract an option for equity purchase if certain conditions or benchmarks are achieved. Giving the agreement more teeth may take some extra effort at the start of the relationship, but it opens the door to substantially greater benefits in the long term.

Joint Venture

The next step up from a marketing alliance is the joint venture (JV), which demands a higher level of commitment from the parties involved. Classically, a JV means the construction of a new entity in which each partner normally has equal ownership. It creates a much higher stake in the outcomes than a marketing alliance, while avoiding the complex issues of buying your partner's company. There are situations where a JV can have significant advantages over a purchase, not only in terms of hard financials but also with respect to the psychology of the partnership.

My firm has a client in the construction industry who needed to grow externally to fill a gap in her technology portfolio. Theoretically, she could have purchased the target company. Psychologically, this would have been a bad move. We were primarily looking for human expertise, meaning we wanted the key people to stay on. With a purchase, this is always in doubt. By setting up a new entity in which the partner had a 50 percent stake, we ensured they had sufficient pride in ownership to be motivated to stay. In the classic JV, neither party is a minority owner, and this feel-good factor can have a significant impact on performance and the longevity of the relationship.

Another case where a joint venture was appropriate concerned a biotechnology company that took a strong interest in a European venture, this time for its market reach. Again, it was essential to our strategy to work with the existing team for some years to come. Our client was far bigger than the target and we were concerned that if the smaller company was simply bought, they would feel railroaded. There is always a tendency for a large company to be overdominant when it makes an acquisition, and sometimes we have to protect our heavyweight clients from themselves. In this case, we set up a JV with 50 percent ownership and 50 percent representation on the board. This meant that the small partner always felt in equal control and was not intimidated by the larger enterprise.

One refinement we added in this case, which can often be fruitful, was to build in the possibility of a later buyout. A joint venture agreement can contain clauses that allow you to take full ownership in the future on terms acceptable to both parties.

Licensing

If you need something that another company owns, one tactic is to acquire the license to use or distribute it. Conversely, licensing your own unique intellectual property to existing companies can be an alternative to buying them.

As a growth tactic, licensing can have the advantage of encouraging high-value people to stay around, which a purchase can jeopardize. By the same token, a licensing agreement poses a problem similar to a strategic alliance. With no equity involvement, what happens when the licensed product reaches the end of its life cycle? What will motivate your partner to create new value or bring you the next great thing?

For your immediate situation, a licensing agreement may be exactly the right tactic. It is especially appropriate if your needs are so specific and limited that a strategic alliance would have no legs. Be sure to compare licensing carefully with the other options being discussed here, however, and if you proceed, look to the future beyond the initial agreement.

Toll Manufacturing

This phrase arose originally in the chemical industry. Toll manufacturing refers simply to an agreement to pay another company to manufacture something you need for your own product or product range. Outsourcing, in other words.

In my own practice, toll manufacturing has rarely been the sole tactic for external growth. It is more often one ingredient in a package of moves. For example, a client may divest a division that is really too far from his core business. But he still needs whatever that division produced, so he goes outside to have it made. Or a purchase is made that meets the client's core growth need and fits his tightly defined criteria, but the target company happens to be deficient in one key element. We fill the gap with toll manufacturing.

This was the direction we took for a client who had acquired a trucking company to strengthen his international distribution. There remained a need for specialist logistics management to get product across frontiers. This was too far from the client's core business, so we simply outsourced it.

One legitimate motive for choosing toll manufacturing over any kind of ownership solution can be to limit liability. This arose for a client in the metal business who needed certain finishing processes that involve extremely hazardous chemicals. Outsourcing that function meant someone else carried the environmental risk, not our client.

Greenfielding

As its name suggests, this is the approach to external growth where you build from scratch. You may or may not literally buy a "green field" and erect a factory. The point is that you use all your own resources to expand, rather than leveraging someone else's.

Often, this tactic is adopted when you choose a road along which to expand but find there is no suitable ally traveling in that direction. For example, we had a client that was providing sophisticated connectivity components for a major U.S. computer manufacturer. They wanted to expand into some related technologies in heat management, leveraging the excellent relationship they had with this one big customer. A stipulation imposed on them was that they had to source their product from what the corporation defined as a low-cost country. So we turned to China, Taiwan, Thailand, and Vietnam in search of a potential acquisition. No one fit, so rather than compromise our strategic criteria, our client decided to build their own plant in Thailand.

Obviously, the greenfield tactic presents its own challenges. The great attraction of an acquisition is that you get an up-and-running operation, whereas building your own can take more time and involve more teething problems. Nevertheless, it is an increasingly common solution, especially in situations like our client's, where low-cost offshore manufacturing is required.

Franchising

Franchising is a field all its own, and there is a well-developed profession of franchise consultants. It is certainly an option to be considered for certain types of products in certain markets, usually consumer-oriented. In effect, franchising provides you with an alternative method of raising capital.

Observing clients and companies that have engaged in franchise activities, we believe there are two unmistakable prerequisites to success. First, a sound franchise operation must have exceptionally well-defined systems. You want to be offering your franchisees a "plug and play" operation that they can get going the moment they assume ownership. So before you even consider the franchise operation, make sure you have a tightly documented and thoroughly tested system for every aspect of the business, from accounting to distribution, from marketing to production, from how the phone is answered to how taxes get filed.

Second, the franchise must have a strong brand. This represents a significant percentage of what the franchisee is paying for. So an essential preparatory step is to invest in a rigorous brand strategy, not just a nice logo. This defines exactly how your company is to be perceived in the marketplace and how that perception is to be managed on every front, including but not limited to the visual presentation.

Needless to say, even if you never franchise, these two steps add value to any enterprise and increase your marketability to both sellers and buyers.

Import/Export

Import and export can be seen as normal tactics of organic growth. I include them in a discussion of external growth for three reasons.

First, the possibilities offered by import/export are often uncovered during the exploration of different options in the Growth Program Review. For example, you may conclude that the best direction is to expand your markets for existing products. You might then review the global possibilities and select one or two target regions. Or using the Michael Porter model, you may decide to protect yourself from excessive dependence on one supplier by seeking alternatives in a foreign country. In both cases, the import/export approach can come into play.

Second, to execute an import or export program, you often need to go out and seek an external partner. Very likely, this partner is located in a foreign country where you lack expertise and connections. For instance, one of our clients searched for someone in Eastern Europe who knew the regulatory and cultural context well enough to provide distribution channels the client needed there. Conversely, another client went to Brazil to reliably source a unique raw material she needed, which she secured on an exclusive basis.

Third, import/export can show up in relation to a larger external growth operation: You may acquire a company that serves a primary function you need but is missing in some secondary elements. Import/export can sometimes fill the gap. You could acquire a company because its technology and personnel allow you to expand your product line, but you may still need to source materials for the planned product from a foreign location. Or you may acquire an operation that adds a valued product but lacks the capabilities to market it effectively abroad. In any of these cases, your import/export tactic serves to complete the picture.

Minority Interest

Before we look at acquisition proper, we should give special consideration to minority interest ownership. This surprisingly neglected tactic has many significant benefits. First, assuming you have limited budget to invest in external growth, buying several minority interests allows you to spread your risks. You don't have to put all your eggs in one basket. Second, you can purchase an interest in a company that would otherwise be too expensive or too big for you to comfortably acquire whole. (See Chapter 3 for some important advice on the size of acquisitions.) A third benefit is that your investment as a minority owner is unlikely to trigger the departure of a management team that you may want to see remain for some years to come.

An instinctive objection arises when we raise the possibility of minority interest purchases with clients: "But we want to control the company we are buying." They think of minority ownership as a kind of passive investment where you effectively have no decision power over what happens.

In reality, you can often have your cake and eat it: You can purchase a minority interest and exercise as much control as is needed to achieve your goals. If there are specific results you are seeking from an acquisition, you can have these written into your minority purchase agreement. They might include customers, suppliers, technology, personnel, or any other asset that is motivating you to make a purchase. If you are looking for more widespread influence, you can also stipulate a substantial presence on the board.

There is another way you can indirectly, but powerfully, exercise control. Build into the agreement the option for purchasing further shares or a complete buyout, and make this option contingent on performance conditions that you set. Walmart uses this strategy extensively. It will buy 30 percent of a manufacturer in China, for example, with an option to purchase the remaining 70 percent when the manufacturer has reached certain production targets. Walmart might stipulate some quite mundane but essential ingredients like getting the factories up to fire code. That way, Walmart doesn't have to manage a difficult situation in an alien territory: It can step in and complete the purchase when the target has evolved to a "Walmart-friendly" condition.

Another value in the minority tactic is that very few potential buyers offer the minority stake option to sellers. This allows you to differentiate yourself when you are competing with other potential partners. The seller gets the benefit of some immediate liquidity while being able to conduct a progressive and orderly exit over time.

Minority ownership has yet another benefit if it leads to acquisition, in that integration is much easier to handle because it is conducted incrementally. You avoid the shock of a sudden union between two different company cultures.

Among the nine pathways of external growth, minority ownership is one tactic you should give special attention to—either as an end in itself or as part of a broader thrust for acquisition.

Acquisition

Here we arrive at the centerpiece of external growth and the topic that consumes the remainder of this book. In the next chapter, we assume that you have elected to buy a company outright, and we begin formulating an acquisition strategy.

My hope is that by this point you have thoroughly considered all the alternatives to acquisition—not because there is anything inherently negative about buying companies. On the contrary, it can often be the single most exciting path to expansion. My point is that every acquisition should be made in the context of a strategic plan that has carefully weighed all possibilities.

If you have followed the process outlined so far, you will have conducted a thorough internal review of your strengths, weaknesses, and growth needs. You will also have looked carefully at a wide range of options for growth, of which external growth is only one. Is your choice to buy a company? If so, then let's move on to Chapter 3 and get started!

CHAPTER 3

PREPARE TO BUY

THE DECISION TO MAKE an acquisition is no small step. Let's assume you have conducted a strategic audit of your business, reviewing where you are, how you got there, and where you want to go. After considering your five pathways to growth (discussed in Chapter 2), you have chosen to expand externally either because you have hit the limits of organic growth or because you have identified clear opportunities for expansion outside your current trajectory. Of the nine approaches to external growth (also discussed in Chapter 2), you have chosen the path of acquisition.

That suggests you recognize the benefits of a "ready-made" solution that a well-executed acquisition can provide. After closing the deal, you can immediately take advantage of new resources at your disposal, such as markets, personnel, ideas, and technology. Needless to say, there is risk inherent in any acquisition, and a great deal of effort is required to achieve a good outcome. But these downsides can pale next to the potentially enormous rewards.

In this chapter, we prepare the ground for your acquisition and provide an overview of the remainder of the acquisition process. Only with thorough planning can you minimize the risks and maximize the rewards of external growth. The process begins by asking a simple yet essential question: *Why acquire?* As we will see, the answer is more complex than simply "to grow." A precise resolution of this question is critical to your success and guides your search for the right company. To start with, we look at what commonly motivates companies to make acquisitions and then consider your situation in terms of what I call the "business puzzle." Next, we take a look at where to begin your search and how to define your initial universe of acquisition prospects. I then introduce the powerful "markets-before-prospects" approach, a hallmark of the Roadmap acquisition process. We also consider the imperative of conducting thorough research before you choose a target company and consider negotiating a deal.

The main message of this chapter is simple: Only rigorous planning enables you to sustain your momentum through the stops and starts of an acquisition process while holding to an objective focus on the issues you are bound to face.

THE TEN MOST COMMON REASONS TO ACQUIRE

We begin by looking for a convincing answer to this question: *What outcomes do you hope to achieve from an acquisition that you could not realize otherwise?* The answer to this lays the strategic foundation on which you build your acquisition process.

For context, let's look at the ten most common reasons that lead companies to embark upon acquisitions:

1. **Increase top-line revenue.** The ultimate objective in any business is higher earnings, and to reach that goal you eventually have to raise your revenues. Cost reduction has diminishing returns and organic growth has its limits, so acquiring a healthy, cash-flowing company can be a powerful route to increased revenues.

2. **Expand in a declining market.** Acquiring a bigger portion of a waning market allows you to maintain or even increase revenues while you wait for the market to rebound. And if it does not rebound, you will at least own a larger slice of a smaller market.

3. **Reverse slippage in market share.** If your company is losing its share of an important market, making an acquisition could stop this slide, as long as you figure out why the slippage is occurring.

4. **Follow your customers.** Your customers may be seeking products or services that you currently do not provide. Adding such products or services to your portfolio through acquisition could give them a "one-stop shop."

5. **Leverage technologies.** Rather than develop a new technology to stay competitive or to spur product innovation, it may be more cost-effective to acquire a company that already owns that technology. Acquisitions give you the unique ability to pick a "winner" among the various versions of a particular technology.

6. **Consolidate.** Acquisition of a company in the same market with the same products or services as your business can increase your purchasing power or reduce redundant expenses by capturing economies of scale.

7. **Stabilize financials.** Buying and incorporating a business with higher margins can bring stability to your balance sheet. When your business is impacted by cyclicality and seasonality, and a cash cow dies, the right acquisition lets you invest in a new breed.

8. **Expand your customer base.** Some corporate customers are tough to penetrate, and having your salespeople try to steal them often just won't work. Acquiring a competitor gives you access to their customer list and the relationships they have built.

9. **Add talent.** Bringing aboard a seasoned executive or dynamic development team from an acquisition adds fresh human resources to your business. Acquiring for this purpose can be seen as a "group hire."

10. **Get defensive.** The best way to fend off competition may be to directly purchase the competitor itself or to buy a valuable company that your rival is positioned to acquire.

Your reason for considering an acquisition is likely to match one of these overall goals. So far, however, this snapshot is too generalized to be useful. We need to relate the broad concepts to your particular situation.

You'll recall that I encouraged you to undertake a strategic audit at the outset of this process. In it, you developed a picture of your company's current profile and where it stands in the marketplace. Then we talked about where you want your company to be in the future: What will your ideal business picture look like in five or ten or even fifteen years? Here, an often neglected key to success is your assessment of future market demand. How will your company satisfy future customers or clients as their needs evolve in the coming years? When you adopt this perspective, you are likely to identify gaps in your current capabilities, resources, or market reach. Future demand is a critical question as you contemplate an acquisition.

DETERMINING THE MISSING PIECE OF THE BUSINESS PUZZLE

My clients have often found it useful to consider the business picture as a puzzle in which some pieces are firmly in place while others are misshaped, incomplete, or missing. These problem pieces represent strategic needs your company must meet in order to realize your future vision, as shown in Figure 3-1.

For example, if you are currently operating in the Northeast and your business vision calls for you to expand to the Midwest, then the "Location" piece of the puzzle is incomplete. Or if your current

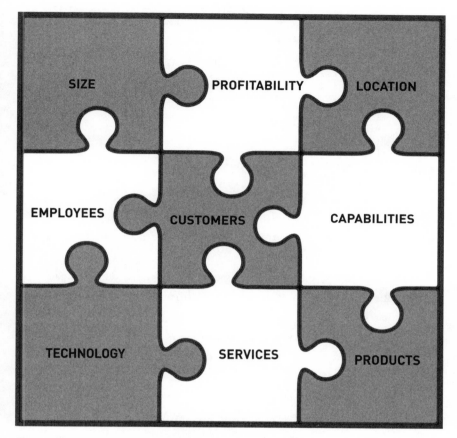

Figure 3-1. The business puzzle.

product line is computer software and your customers are migrating to mobile devices, then "Technology" becomes a critical piece.

Let me give another example from my firm's experience. A client of ours in the food business conducted a strategic audit and realized they were dependent on commodity seafood—simply raising and selling shrimp. In their vision for the future of the company, they wanted more product breadth. For their business puzzle, the "Products" piece was out of line. To fill this gap, they pursued and acquired a company that made frozen Asian entrees—with shrimp, of course! Our client also decided to diversify into organic seafood.

These moves eventually led to a contract as a supplier to Whole Foods, the world's largest retailer of natural and organic foods. The "Products" piece of their business puzzle was now complete, and as a secondary consequence, they were able to enhance the "Customers" piece, too.

HAVE ONE REASON TO BUY

Assuming you have determined to use acquisition to fuel your growth, now is the time to look closely at your own business puzzle. What strategic needs are demanding to be met? Most likely, you will discover several.

I strongly believe that each of your strategic needs, each piece of the puzzle—whether it is location, technology, customers, talent, finance, or something else—requires a separate acquisition strategy. In other words, every time you head down the path of acquisition, you should be looking to identify and meet just *one* strategic need with each company you buy.

Think of how you go about hiring new employees. If you have simultaneous needs in sales, accounting, and operations, you are not going to hire one person to fill all three spots. The qualifications for each position are unique and you look for three different individuals to fill those roles.

The same concept applies to making an acquisition. Having a single, clear purpose for an acquisition keeps you focused on which markets to look at and which companies to consider. If you try to make one company fulfill multiple needs, you embark on a dangerous path that blurs your decision making. The risk is that you'll find ways to justify acquiring almost any target you select. This is exactly the kind of vague thinking that leads to bad acquisitions and problematic integration. Although it may seem that killing two birds with one stone is cost-effective, it is likely to prove far more expensive in the long run. Trying to fulfill multiple needs through one acquisition meets none of them well.

Think back in time to the infamous AOL–Time Warner merger, now widely judged a failure. The original press release issued to announce the deal is very revealing. Here's what it said: "No company will be able to better capitalize on the convergence of entertainment, communications, and commerce. . . . The possibilities are truly endless. The true value of this union lies not in what it will do today, but what it will do in the future."

While possibilities are endless, actualities can be avoided. AOL–Time Warner fell victim to an undisciplined strategic approach. Lacking a single, specific rationale, the merger became that most dangerous and wasteful animal: a solution in search of a problem.

Contrast the announcement above with a quote from a press release that a client of mine, a German manufacturer, released after we helped them acquire an American competitor: "This acquisition will allow [us] to accelerate our growth strategy to manufacture and distribute our products in the U.S. market."

No glowing rhetoric here, but the reason for acquisition is clear: Expand the customer base by entering a new geographic market. Unlike the more spectacular AOL–Time Warner merger, this has been a successful and profitable marriage.

Singularity gives focus, and focus generates results. You may be able to read by a diffuse light, but you need a laser beam to cut through steel. Our German client identified a single need and adopted a focused acquisition strategy—and they were successful because of it. If you are determined to achieve a profitable result, be sure to follow this fundamental rule as you prepare for acquisition: Have only one reason to buy.

PREPARING TO SEARCH

Let's take a step back and review where you are in your preparations. At this point you have:

- Made a thorough examination of your business

- Developed a vision of what you want your company to look like in order to meet future demand

- Determined what your company requires in order to fulfill that vision—the missing pieces in your business puzzle

- Identified which strategic need you are going to focus on— your one reason for making the current acquisition

Now it is time to begin the search for the right company to meet your selected need.

The scale of your projected acquisition is an important question you need to settle early on. Your objective is growth, and it would be easy to deduce from this that the bigger your purchase, the better. Not so. You've heard the familiar question "How do you eat an elephant?" with the equally familiar answer, "One bite at a time." That's the optimum mindset to adopt when strategizing your external growth. It is dangerous to try to expand too far too fast, or to make a quantum leap by acquiring a company much larger than your own. A series of small acquisitions gives you a better chance that each one will tightly fit the need it is supposed to meet. Your acquisitions will also be easier to integrate and assimilate into your company's culture—a critical stage of the process that we explore in Chapter 13.

Another primary question to address is whether to restrict your search to companies that are advertising themselves as "for sale." It may seem obvious to consider companies that are actively seeking a buyer. This is indeed the most common procedure and one that is widely advocated by investment bankers. However, it is an approach that severely limits your chances of finding the right company. Companies are often for sale for a reason. Whether the reason is financial difficulty or ownership problems, it can make these targets much less attractive. Also, with for-sale companies, there are often multiple potential buyers (including your competitors), which may drive up the price. This can shift the balance of power to the seller. Finally, the inventory of for-sale companies can dry up quickly, leaving you with too few options and backing you into the corner of trying to make an inappropriate company fit your one chosen need.

PURSUING THE NOT-FOR-SALE ADVANTAGE

When a company is "not for sale," that simply means it isn't actively seeking a buyer. If through your search and screening process you discover a company that could be the right fit for your acquisition criteria, then it should be pursued, even if it is ostensibly not for sale.

The central point here is that *every* company is for sale—for the right equation. "Equation" usually means more than price. It can include timing, ownership, reputation, vision, location, and a host of other factors related to the owner's values and aspirations. Later, we delve much deeper into how to put that equation together. For now, the crucial point is not to exclude any company simply because it isn't wearing a "for-sale" sign. If you find a company that you believe is the best candidate to meet your chosen strategic need, then my advice is simple: Go after it. In fact, the rest of this book is primarily focused on helping you find the best "not-for-sale" candidates.

Pursuing not-for-sale companies holds several significant advantages. It puts you in a proactive, rather than a reactive, position, allowing you to choose what you want. The management team of a not-for-sale company is actively engaged in the business, not eyeing the exits. Often, the managers are eager to stay on (if you want them to) after the deal is done. Another benefit of looking at not-for-sale companies is that you can maintain stealth in the marketplace, allowing you to pursue an acquisition that no one else knows about. It also lets you avoid the auction process, which often drives good people out and prices up.

DEVELOPING FUNDAMENTAL CRITERIA FOR FILTERING PROSPECTS

By including not-for-sale companies in your search, you have significantly expanded your universe of potential acquisition prospects. With such a large pool, you must develop criteria through which to filter the prospects in order to narrow your options. Although you have one reason to make the purchase, you should have several criteria for vetting potential buys.

The first step in establishing your criteria for prospects is to review your strategic audit, taking into consideration each fundamental aspect of your business: marketing, production, distribution, management, sales, accounting, etc. Your acquisition criteria should take each of these core functions into account.

Throughout this book, you will find me imploring you to return to your criteria when you reach an impasse in the decision-making process. Criteria become an objective touch point for you throughout the entire acquisition process. There are no "right" or "wrong" criteria. They are simply whatever you value in a market or company to address your one reason for growth.

SELECTING MARKETS FIRST

Once you have identified your target criteria, it would seem the logical next step is to go looking for individual companies. This is premature. Before selecting prospective acquisitions, there is one critical question that must be settled: Which markets should you focus on? "Markets" here might be defined geographically, vertically, or by any other factor appropriate to your industry.

There are compelling reasons for researching markets before individual companies, derived from the "demand-driven" philosophy of growth I have already advocated. You might find a wonderful company with strong financials, but if it is operating in a shrinking market where the future demand for its products and services looks unpromising, you risk buying a lemon. In other words, the focus on markets is really a focus on future demand—specifically on demand that you and your new partner can confidently meet.

Market selection should begin with a broad sweep but become progressively narrower. You will eventually be looking for very specific segments, because the tighter your market focus, the greater your chances of success. If your approach to markets is geographic, for example, you may begin by considering an acquisition in Europe. But as your research deepens, you may find yourself looking only in southern Germany. If you are looking to acquire an auto parts manufacturer, you may narrow your focus to those that make parts for hybrid cars instead of for all vehicles. Again, your pick of specific markets and segments should be based on your anticipation of future demand.

Researching and selecting your markets also allows you to establish a large yet relevant choice of possible acquisition prospects. You begin by identifying the major players in your chosen market, and then you uncover companies that you may not have considered.

Finally, the work you do developing criteria to select the right market and understanding the market dynamics helps you enormously when it comes to evaluating individual prospects. For example, if customers in a particular market are trending toward a certain technology, you ensure that any company you consider possesses the technology that meets that growing demand.

Chapter 5 goes into great detail on how to research and select markets. In that chapter, I help you establish market criteria and give you tips for research. Using criteria to choose markets is just as vital as using them for prospects. It gives you an objective reference point to return to when deciding which markets to enter. For now, our priority is to establish why you first research and select markets before going after individual prospects.

COMMITTING TO RESEARCH

Clearly, to find the company that best meets your strategic need, you must commit to doing the necessary research. Only thorough research uncovers the most appropriate markets, helps you identify the best prospects, and sets you apart from other potential buyers.

There are two levels of research to consider. The easier kind is secondary research, drawing from public sources such as the Internet. Secondary research enables you to explore market size, growth rates, supply chains, and other market dynamics. This is an essential requisite that prepares you for conducting the more difficult but more rewarding primary research. Here, you get on the phone and talk to a variety of industry players and observers about the market, industry trends, and, where possible, your acquisition prospects.

We discuss specific research strategies for markets in Chapter 5 and for prospects in Chapter 6. At this planning stage, understanding the importance of research ensures that you and your team are committed throughout the rest of the process.

HOW LONG WILL IT TAKE?

One of the most frequent questions I hear when laying out an acquisition plan is: *How long will this whole process take?* The answer is never easy to pin down. I've worked on acquisitions that were completed in a month, while others took years to finish. Generally speaking, if you are starting from scratch and following the steps laid out in this book, you should be able to close on your first acquisition within twelve to eighteen months. If you push any faster, it is unlikely that you will have time to do the necessary research and examine a sufficient volume of markets and prospects. (See Figure 3-2 for a typical timeline for an acquisition.)

Many factors impact the time frame, including the size of the target, the complexity of the transaction, and the psychology of the

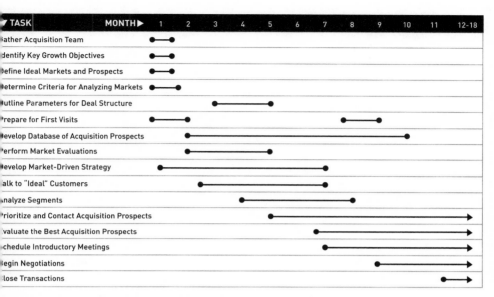

TASK	MONTH▶	1	2	3	4	5	6	7	8	9	10	11	12-18
Gather Acquisition Team		●—●											
Identify Key Growth Objectives		●—●											
Define Ideal Markets and Prospects		●—●											
Determine Criteria for Analyzing Markets		●—●											
Outline Parameters for Deal Structure				●————●									
Prepare for First Visits		●—●						●———●					
Develop Database of Acquisition Prospects			●————————————————●										
Perform Market Evaluations			●———●										
Develop Market-Driven Strategy		●————————————●											
Talk to "Ideal" Customers			●————————●									
Analyze Segments				●————————●								
Prioritize and Contact Acquisition Prospects					●——————————————⟶							
Evaluate the Best Acquisition Prospects						●————————————⟶						
Schedule Introductory Meetings						●————————————⟶						
Begin Negotiations									●————⟶				
Close Transactions												●—⟶	

Figure 3-2. A typical acquisition timeline.

parties involved. Another factor is your own level of decisiveness. Adopting the Roadmap approach, which is based on dozens of real-world acquisitions, should give you confidence to pull the trigger and make the right acquisition when the opportunity appears. I still have clients who are hesitant to act or who enjoy the dance more than closing the deal, but speed of decision making obviously impacts the time it takes to complete an acquisition.

The fundamentals we have discussed in this chapter may appear like common sense, yet they are remarkably *un*common in the real world of M&A. If you embrace them, you will separate yourself from the majority of players in the acquisition game and hugely increase your chances of a successful outcome. Of course, principles alone never deliver a result. You need the right people to put those principles into action, and that is the focus of the next chapter.

CHAPTER 4

ASSEMBLING YOUR A-TEAM

YOUR PLAN TO BUY, no matter how well crafted, is only as good as the people who execute it. Acquisition is a team sport for two reasons. Practically speaking, buying a company involves multiple skills—more than any single individual could possess. Just as important, successful growth requires multiple perspectives. You need to see the opportunities and risks of a potential purchase from many points of view.

In this chapter, we take a close look at your acquisition team—what I call the "A-Team." When should it be formed? What are the key roles? Who needs to be included? What is the leader's function? How does the CEO fit in? These are just some of the questions we address.

ACQUISITION IS A COLLABORATIVE EFFORT

First, we might do well to look at how acquisition teams are usually assembled and how the Roadmap approach I'm advocating is different from standard industry practice. Everyone who embarks on a company purchase knows—or quickly discovers—what a wide range of expertise is required. Of course, the skills involved are not needed all at once. Early on, for example, your focus is research. Then, once a target has been selected, you need great negotiators and people who can appraise a company's value. Due diligence draws you into more technical accounting waters, and then there are all the legal aspects that must be handled. Finally, special management expertise is demanded to achieve a successful integration of the two entities involved. What usually happens is that each of the requisite experts is engaged as and when needed, and then slips out of the picture. In other words, there never really is a "team" in the sense of a consistently active group of people focused on a common goal. Instead, a succession of players comes and goes under the direction of one or two executives.

The lack of coordination and single vision that results from this habitual practice is one of the prime reasons so many acquisitions end in failure. Imagine an orchestral concert in which the players keep drifting on and off the stage to play their part of the symphony. There would be no cohesion, no theme—in fact, no music.

When I undertake an acquisition for a client, I always insist on this principle: The entire acquisition team will be recruited right at the beginning, and every key player will be involved throughout the entire process—in other words, "from beginning to beginning." Our A-Team is more than a succession of experts: It's a brain trust, a mastermind forum for decision making that develops a collective understanding of the whole acquisition process.

ASSESSING IN-HOUSE RESOURCES

The first step in forming the acquisition team is to conduct an assessment of your in-house acquisition expertise. You need to be careful not to confuse "experience" with expertise. You may have people in your company who have been through a number of acquisitions. They may even have led an acquisition team. But unless they have followed the step-by-step Roadmap approach we are exploring here, that history could end up being a hindrance to your acquisition plans.

I have found the contrast of experience with expertise to be particularly evident among private equity groups (PEGs). Often, their main focus is to get a deal done as quickly as possible. This philosophy does not lend itself to a systematic acquisition process and threatens to produce a poor outcome for the long term. There are people who have a significant number of acquisitions on their resume but have learned surprisingly little about what makes an acquisition successful. A prime example is a private equity client I had who would often tell me, "That's a great company you've found for us, but if they aren't willing to sell immediately, we won't look at them." This client had completed many acquisitions and therefore had lots of so-called experience—but too many of the purchases were unsuccessful. The past disappointments are no mystery: My PEG client lacked patience and refused to go after companies that were not actively searching for buyers. Even with their years of M&A activity, they failed to understand that every company is for sale for the right equation if, and only if, the buyer shows the patience to discover it.

Most likely you will find that your in-house team has many real skills but little expertise approaching acquisitions with the Roadmap approach that focuses on not-for-sale companies. This is not a cause for concern but rather an opportunity. You have a chance here to mold (or remold) your team to embrace a truly strategic outlook. With everyone starting from the same page, it will be easier to form a consensus moving forward.

BUILDING THE INTERNAL TEAM

Your acquisition team should consist of a mixture of people drawn from the ranks of your company and experts engaged from outside. Having gauged the level of M&A know-how in your organization, you can start to build your internal team.

The first step is to win the commitment of your CEO and/or company board to making an acquisition based on your single strategic need. This may sometimes be difficult but is essential to the remainder of the acquisition process. A strong commitment from the top empowers your team and gives its members confidence that their efforts will have a definite outcome—that an acquisition will be made. Tepid support can discourage bold choices and in the process lead to stagnation. What you need from the CEO is a signal of willingness to entertain the unavoidable risks of external growth—a signal that you can reinforce if your team starts becoming overly risk-averse.

Support from the CEO must include complete alignment with the end result that you and your acquisition team have defined. Think of building a home. If you simply say, "I am building a house" to ten different people, they will each have ten different visions of what that house will look like. They understand the concept—building a structure for shelter—but will have different plans and blueprints to get there. Commitment from the CEO entails adopting a shared vision of what the team is working toward.

With strong backing from the top, you can move forward with selecting your internal acquisition team. The first person to appoint is your Acquisition Coordinator, who functions (in football terms) as the team's quarterback. The Acquisition Coordinator's job is to manage the process and drive it forward. This key individual usually has another job title in your organization, such as CFO or director of business development, and therefore carries other important responsibilities. Nevertheless, he should expect to spend a minimum of 50 percent of his time on the acquisition process: Anything less, and it will be impossible to effectively lead the team.

One essential point about the Acquisition Coordinator must be established here. The role should not be taken by the CEO. This may seem counterintuitive but is based on long experience. You need a team composed of strong individuals willing to question every idea, challenge each other's positions, and ruthlessly jettison approaches that don't add up. If the Acquisition Coordinator role is taken by the CEO, on whose decisions careers may depend, other team members are unlikely to speak and act freely. For this reason, the CEO should not even be a member of the A-Team.

Experience has taught me that there is a far more constructive role for your company's leader to play. Like the king on a chessboard, the CEO has symbolic power in the process. In the eyes of both the acquisition team and the seller, your CEO is the critical decision maker; just as in dealings between nations, subordinates conduct the backroom dealings while presidents take the major initiatives. Likewise in the acquisition process, the CEO should step in only to lend special authority at a critical moment. For example, if the Acquisition Coordinator cannot resolve an impasse in the team's decision making, an intervention from the top may be needed. Similarly, if a crisis occurs in negotiations with the seller, the prestige of the CEO may provide the key to a resolution. The CEO can inject new energy into the process whenever a roadblock pops up.

With the Acquisition Coordinator in place, you can now enroll the other players. A distinction in the Roadmap approach is the functional team structure. It would be natural to imagine that the team would be organized in terms of M&A skills. In reality, I have found it more effective for the team members to represent each of the primary areas of your company: production, sales, marketing, financial, legal, human resources, and so on. Note that the representative may be the head of a department but does not have to be. Each company function will be impacted by the acquisition, and each has unique insights that can help form a sound judgment of a target's appropriateness or value.

Even if your acquisition strategy focuses on just one of these areas, having a team member from each department prevents "silo thinking." Let's imagine that your strategic need is to obtain a new technology that will primarily benefit production. Each of the other areas is still affected, though some more than others. Human resources must consider the technical qualifications of current employees and future hires, legal might have to worry about intellectual property issues, and sales will have to figure out how to alter the sales strategy once the new technology becomes available.

TEAM DYNAMICS: AN UNUSUAL MANAGEMENT CHALLENGE

An acquisition team is unlike any other team that you have operating in your company. The responsibilities placed on its members are likely to be larger and more demanding than any they have assumed in the past. Buying another company is a massive undertaking, with complex ramifications for the future of the enterprise. Most of your employees are accustomed to delivering information and advice to a higher decision maker, rather than shouldering decisions themselves. They are more used to being like aides to a state governor than actually holding the reins of power. For those new to the process, the fear of "screwing up" can bring it to a grinding halt, so there may be some training required to support the team in fully taking on its responsibilities and freedom of action.

For a successful outcome, the A-Team must observe certain ground rules. When a decision is needed, it is important to arrive at a genuine agreement among the team members, like a jury acting in a legal trial. That means that once a decision is arrived at, everyone is fully committed to it. Unity of agreement gives the team authority throughout the rest of the company, and some hard battles may need to be fought along the way to a purchase. While the acquisition team is by no means a democracy, there is a requirement for every member to clearly voice decisive opinions. When the crunch comes, no one can sit on the fence. No one can hide.

SKEPTICS AND OPTIMISTS

When you assemble the A-Team, you are likely to find yourself with a group of diverse personalities. In my experience, these personalities generally fall into one of two groups: skeptics and optimists. Understanding this distinction is one of the keys to success.

The skeptics usually come from the financial side of the business—the "bean counters," trained to conserve resources and minimize risk. While these qualities are admirable in the day-to-day practice of financial management, they can be detrimental during the acquisition process if they are left unchecked. Skepticism can reach a point where fear of risk paralyzes your team and renders it incapable of action.

The optimists typically come from sales and marketing. Great salespeople are inherently upbeat and have a tendency to believe their own stories. That's actually what makes them so convincing! Again, this is an admirable quality in its own place, but in an acquisition scenario, optimists may develop blind spots for companies that look attractive, missing fatal flaws that lie just underneath the surface.

To avoid risk-averse skeptics or delusional optimists overrunning your acquisition process, you need a good mix of the two, allowing them to temper each other. On balance, the skeptics tend to be the most problematic because they are by nature avoiders of action. The danger in giving them too much sway is that they can paralyze the entire acquisition process. Optimists are constantly in motion: They simply need steering in the right direction. Either way, you always benefit from including people who adapt easily when there are bumps in the road that threaten morale. They can remind the team of its commitment to the process and sustain a constant focus on the end results: buying the best company to fill the identified need.

THE ACQUISITION COORDINATOR AS CHAMPION

Healthy debate, of the kind you can expect in a well-balanced team, does not mean making everyone happy. There are times for the talking to stop and action to be taken. That can require strong leadership from the Acquisition Coordinator and occasionally may call for intervention from the CEO. With the potential for personality con-flicts and emotionally charged decision making, as well as the danger of bureaucratic stasis, the Acquisition Coordinator has a crucial role to play as the champion for the program. Passion is an essential ingredient of successful acquisitions, but there's an important dis-tinction here. The Acquisition Coordinator should be a passionate advocate of the process and its goal—not of any market or target company in particular. The role of champion is to provide overall direction to the team, keeping members informed of what is going on, pushing through roadblocks, and moving everyone forward toward a successful outcome.

The Acquisition Coordinator is responsible for keeping a bal-ance in the team's deliberations, making sure that everyone is heard and that no one dominates. Another key function is to avoid the group mind from closing in too quickly on an attractive solution by keeping multiple options open on the table for consideration. The champion presses the team to remember the agreed criteria and ensures that potential targets are measured against these objective standards. It's the criteria that protect the process from being driven by impulse, anxiety, or wishful thinking. When consensus becomes difficult to reach, the Acquisition Coordinator makes the final call on when and how to move to the next step.

The Acquisition Coordinator is also the primary liaison with the seller. We explore buyer-seller relations in depth later, but for now, suffice it to say that the champion, as the main point of contact with the seller, must be well versed in the seller's motivations and concerns.

The champion's biggest role is to always bring the team back to the foundations of the agreed acquisition strategy. The A-Team's commitment to that strategy will be decisive for the outcome of the process. The Acquisition Coordinator is the jealous guardian of your one reason to buy.

BUILDING THE EXTERNAL TEAM

Unless yours is a very large publicly traded company, you are unlikely to find in your own ranks all the expertise needed to complete a successful acquisition. You probably need to enhance your A-Team with outside specialists. Typically, the external team is drawn from the following professionals:

- **Lawyers**—assist in putting together the legal structure of the deal and tackle other legal questions such as liability issues.

- **Accountants**—handle the financial details and capital issues, as well as the tax implications that sometimes form a central component of the deal structure.

- **Valuation experts**—apply complex algorithms to bring a measure of objectivity to assessing a target company's worth.

- **Due diligence experts**—examine the seller from a number of perspectives, such as accounting, legal, marketing, technical, and environmental, and report back on risks associated with those areas.

- **Third-party acquisition adviser**—acts as a guide through the entire process, taking on tasks such as strategy development, market and prospect research, making first contact with owners, and guiding the negotiations.

- **Investment bankers**—provide you with leads to companies that are looking to be bought and may also help you to come up with the money to finish the deal.

The more integrated the external players are with the internal team, the better. They should really be seen as part of the A-Team rather than as miscellaneous appendages. That means that you benefit from recruiting the key outsiders early in the process and exposing them to your strategic thinking. Enroll your external consultants in the vision, not just the technicalities, and hold them to the same objective criteria that your internal team members are committed to.

DO YOU NEED A THIRD-PARTY ADVISER?

Of the external team positions listed above, the third-party adviser may seem the most optional. The need for lawyers and accountants is self-evident, while an acquisition adviser might look like "just another consultant"—nice to have if resources allow, but easily dispensable.

In reality, the third-party adviser may prove to be a vital member of your team. The clue here lies in the phrase "third-party." Despite its enormous technical complexity, a company acquisition is always an emotionally loaded enterprise for both buyer and seller. And as I have stressed, it needs to be. Without a level of passionate involvement, the job simply won't get done. There is so much at stake on both sides. The buyer is undertaking a major though calculated risk in pursuit of significant growth, while the seller may well be letting go of a lifetime's creation—a personal legacy as well as a massive financial asset.

Having someone at your side with no emotional attachments— someone who brings years of transaction experience and remains coolly objective throughout the process—can be more than a help. The adviser can be the salvation of an otherwise intractable deal.

The third-party adviser can help you develop your acquisition strategy in the first place, guiding you to find a path to external growth that optimally serves your business goals. Then, once the ball starts rolling, your adviser becomes the guardian of that same strategy, steering your A-Team back to the fundamentals when fires break out and team members panic. You could say that the adviser is your champion's champion, maintaining vision, morale, clarity of thinking, and focus on the outcome.

Beyond this, the third-party adviser can play an irreplaceable role in the research process. With the advantage of anonymity, she can engage in conversations with key players in the relevant market space, talking to vendors, competitors, influencers, and the targets themselves to uncover vital intelligence. Throughout this essential discovery journey, you have not yet shown your hand as a potential buyer.

Once the time comes to directly approach a potential target and initiate the courtship, your third-party adviser has the skills to get through the door and then open the conversation without provoking a preemptive "no." This is especially relevant when pursuing not-for-sale companies. If you have a third party make the first contact, you can stay out of the picture while gauging the owner's interest in selling. Your adviser can begin building the owner's trust and then introduce you when the time is right.

The third-party acquisition adviser can also serve as a "marriage counselor" through the negotiation phase. There are bound to be rough spots on the road to any acquisition agreement, and although the adviser is beholden to you, she can provide a trusted ear for both sides. I have found that an expert third party can act as a lightning rod for any negative energy that the seller might have, such as doubt, anxiety, and frustration. The seller needs an avenue to express those feelings but may be uncomfortable talking to someone who could be his future boss or partner. The third-party adviser provides the perfect outlet for these feelings and disperses them, minimizing any potential damage to the relationship between buyer and seller.

Let's again remember that most acquisitions end in failure. From my perspective of largely successful acquisitions, the missing piece in many of these stories is the presence of an "outside insider" who can unearth hidden intelligence, resolve stubborn conflicts, help cooler heads prevail, and maintain a strategic perspective from beginning to beginning.

Your relationship with a third-party adviser requires a delicate balance. You are outsourcing to the adviser for help, but you cannot abdicate leadership to her because of your lesser expertise. The adviser is there to counsel and assist you in the acquisition process, not perform it for you. The critical decisions remain yours alone.

LET THE SEARCH BEGIN

So now your acquisition plan is in place and your A-Team is assembled with the right mix of skills and personalities, from both inside and outside your organization. You are ready to start the search for the optimum target company, beginning with the right market to focus on. The next chapter prepares you to find that ideal market, within which lies the best company to fill your one reason for acquisition.

CHAPTER 5

RESEARCHING AND
SELECTING A MARKET

IN CHAPTER 3, I introduced what I called the "markets first" approach to searching for acquisition targets. The idea is that before you look for a company to buy, you define the market in which you are going to conduct your search. The reason for first selecting a market is to ensure that there is a healthy, stable demand for your acquisition partner's products or services. Without that certainty, you have reason to beware of even the most tempting buying opportunity. A sweet-smelling prospect in a no-growth market may well turn out to be a lemon. The fact is that in almost every business situation, growth follows demand.

Researching and selecting the right market to enter marks the final step in the *Build the Foundations* phase of your external growth program. Once this is complete, you are ready to embark on a focused search for the optimum target companies. In this chapter, we discuss how to find the most promising market using an objective, criteria-based approach. As always, we start out from your reason to buy: your single overriding goal in making an acquisition. Using simple but proven analytic tools, we decide in which market the best opportunity lies to reach that one objective. We pay special attention to establishing the right criteria to guide your choice, such as market size, growth rate, and the status of major players. We conclude with a close look at the research activity itself, including realistic outcomes to pursue and the best methods for achieving your research goals.

GUIDING PRINCIPLES

Your search for the right market should be guided by a few basic principles. First, you must determine how you want to define "market"—geographically, vertically, or whatever makes the most sense for your particular industry. Second, market selection begins with a broad sweep and then progressively zeroes in on individual segments. This maximizes the chances of success, as demand can vary within a broadly defined market. Thorough research will reveal the likely future demand for each segment, increasing your chances of finding the right company to leverage that demand. Third, although your focus is markets, not companies, you are likely to come across individual companies of interest as you conduct your research, so it is important to keep track of them. Finally, just as you establish criteria for assessing markets, you will later build another set of criteria for identifying target companies. The work that goes into choosing the right market and understanding its dynamics will enormously help you in refining the criteria for your ideal prospect—a topic we will cover extensively in Chapter 6.

A pertinent example of the power of the "markets first" philosophy can be seen in one of my clients, a publicly traded specialty engineering company making products for the thermal management market. When I first met with them, they had become a conglomerate of loosely connected companies that touched on many different segments within their overall market. As a result, they had a presence in various fields but were not recognized as a leader in any of them. This situation had arisen over the previous few years while they were working with a New York investment bank that was bringing only for-sale deals to the table from disparate market segments. Management, feeling they needed to be a "player" in every area, readily snatched up these miscellaneous acquisitions, even though they lacked clear strategic value.

One executive, a division vice president, realized this approach wasn't bearing fruit. Working with him, we began the search for a market where his company could be recognized as a clear leader. After scanning more than thirty markets, specifically exploring their thermal needs, we saw an opportunity in the area of active thermal management, where temperature needs to be controlled within a very small margin, sometimes down to hundredths of a degree. We found a particular need in high-end markets such as the pharmaceutical, medical research, and aerospace industries, and we discovered that no single company was considered the go-to provider for all active thermal management needs.

It became clear that this presented an opportunity to make my client the preeminent thermal management company in a defined segment. Through our continued research, we narrowed the field further. We found that a particular technology—thermal electric chillers, a type of specialized portable air conditioner—was vital to the high-end market. Our client's first acquisition was in this area, and they have continued to look to add niche players across the spectrum of active thermal management as they establish themselves as leaders in the field.

It should be clear from that success why I emphasize to my clients the enormous value of painstaking market research and selection before considering individual prospects. If you follow this path, you immediately separate yourself from the majority of company buyers and place yourself at an important competitive advantage. Using the tools that follow, you will be equipped to conduct a thorough and efficient hunt for the best market in which to locate your ideal prospect. Let's get started!

THE OPPORTUNITY MATRIX

Finding the optimum market begins by looking for where the best opportunities lie—where future demand will be the strongest. To that end, I have developed a simple but extremely effective tool called the Opportunity Matrix (see Figure 5-1). It takes the form of a two-by-two grid: The vertical axis is for products and services, while the horizontal axis is for markets and customers. The grid enables you to assess both existing and future demand, a critical distinction as we are especially concerned about future growth.

To make use of the Opportunity Matrix, you focus on your cho-

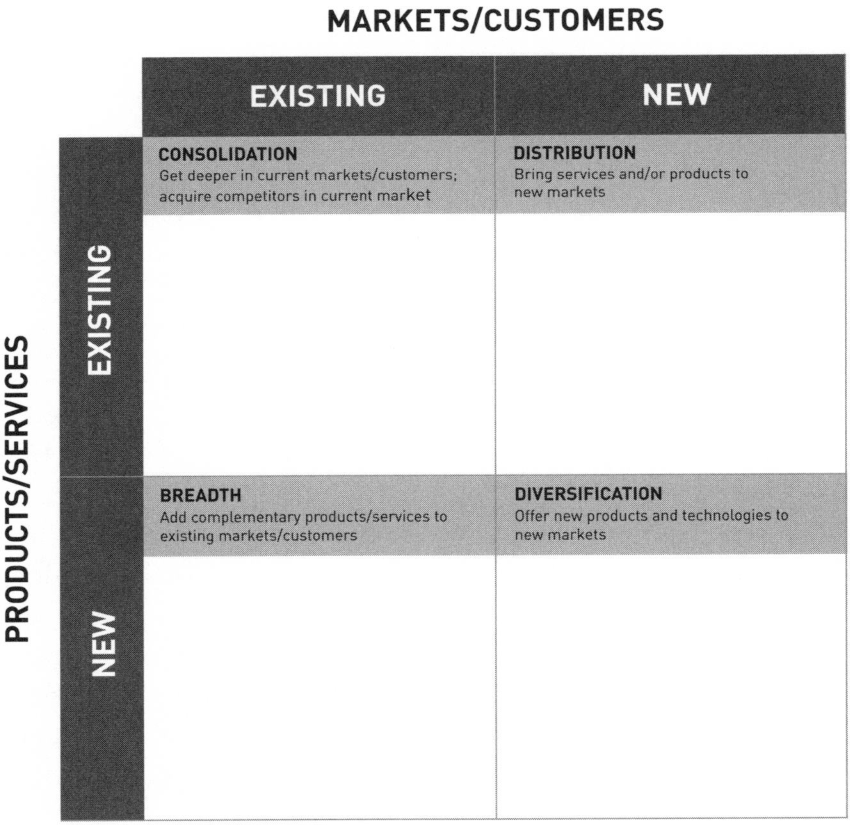

MARKETS/CUSTOMERS

	EXISTING	NEW
EXISTING	**CONSOLIDATION** Get deeper in current markets/customers; acquire competitors in current market	**DISTRIBUTION** Bring services and/or products to new markets
NEW	**BREADTH** Add complementary products/services to existing markets/customers	**DIVERSIFICATION** Offer new products and technologies to new markets

(PRODUCTS/SERVICES)

Figure 5-1. The Opportunity Matrix.

sen reason for making an acquisition—that all-important single goal. You ask yourself: "Where does our objective belong in this matrix?" Let's consider some examples:

- If you are looking to acquire a direct competitor to capture additional market share, your objective falls in the upper left —existing markets, existing products or services. This is *consolidation*, typically the least risky quadrant.

- If you are looking to offer your current product range to new markets, you are in the upper right quadrant. *Distribution* is bringing your existing competencies to new markets.

- If your goal is to bring new products or services to customers in the markets you are already serving, you are in the lower left quadrant, adding *breadth*.

- If your vision of growth is to offer new products or services to markets that you are not already serving, you find yourself in the lower right quadrant: *diversification*. This is the riskiest quadrant because it takes you outside your current knowledge of either products or markets.

Once the Opportunity Matrix is filled in, it is used to determine priorities. Where you find yourself on this grid helps you decide where to begin your market search. If you are consolidating or adding breadth, you naturally begin by looking at the markets where you are already a player. If you are seeking to distribute your current services or diversify, you need to research markets where you do not currently have a toehold.

The power of the Opportunity Matrix lies in its simplicity. It organizes many different perspectives and factors into a single logical focus, bringing objectivity to your planning.

To begin your search, you and your A-Team can brainstorm possible markets, depending on where your acquisition objective falls in the Opportunity Matrix. Once you have a starting list of markets, you need to prioritize them so you maximize your research resources. You want to gather highly detailed information on only the most attractive markets and their segments. This prioritization is achieved through the application of market criteria, which we explore next.

BUILDING YOUR CRITERIA

Carefully defining your market criteria brings further discipline and objectivity to the research process. Your criteria should be rooted in your singular acquisition goal. The long-term growth plans of your enterprise should always be the determining forces as you focus in, first on markets and then on target companies. It's the responsibility of the A-Team to build your search criteria with the big picture in mind, and to arrive at a consensus that will be consistently adhered to in the face of distracting excitements or demoralizing anxieties. There are no inherently "right" or "wrong" criteria; yours should include whatever you value in a market to address the needs of your company's strategic growth initiative.

Here are some guidelines for building effective market selection criteria, based on years of practice with clients in a variety of industries:

- **Focus on strategic aspects early.** For example, if your one reason for acquiring is to bring a current competency to a new market, you want to make sure that whatever new market you buy into is growing sufficiently. In this case, growth rate should be one of your earliest criteria.

- **Be realistic about the availability of information.** You may not be able to immediately get growth rates for the last twenty years or sales figures for the previous year. As you progress, you will gather increasing detail about the market (and individual prospects), but in the beginning, you can make do with relatively broad information.

- **Limit to no more than six criteria.** If you have more than six criteria, you can lose focus on the most meaningful strategic aspects. However, each individual criterion may have multiple metrics. For example, the criterion "customers" may include the size of the customer base, switching costs, and geographic distribution, among others.

- **Make it measurable.** When conducting your research, establishing target metrics for each criterion gives more power and focus to your decision-making process. It is more useful to say that you seek a market with a growth rate of at least 8 percent rather than just a market that has "strong growth."

COMMON CRITERIA

While it is true that any relevant factors can form your search criteria, there are some that prove common to most market searches that I have conducted for clients.

Market Size and Segmentation

Market size (usually measured in dollars of revenue) is almost always a significant criterion because it provides the initial indication of growth opportunity. However, bigger is not necessarily better, and you may find greater success in a smaller, niche market. So the criterion of size needs to be considered in relation to other factors.

The question of market size leads us to consider market segmentation. As I have mentioned, you would do best to begin by researching and prioritizing broadly defined markets and then focus in on individual segments in the highest priority markets. In this way, your market research phase passes through multiple rounds as a broadly defined market becomes segmented and possibly sub-segmented.

My firm once had a client that provided services to individuals with disabilities. Their business had specifically focused on individuals with developmental problems such as autism, but they realized that the services they offered could be applicable to a wider range of people needing help with daily activities. They decided the best growth path was to acquire providers in directly related service areas in order to expand their client population. In other words, they chose to take their existing competencies into new markets—the distribution quadrant of the Opportunity Matrix (upper right).

This client followed the Roadmap approach precisely. Before identifying individual target companies, we conducted an analysis of potential markets. In this case, market criteria included funding sources, customer needs, market dynamics, and market size and growth. First we applied the criteria to macro markets such as childcare facilities, family support, special education, and senior housing. The most promising market turned out to be senior housing, which we then broke down into niche segments—independent living, assisted living, nursing homes, and so on. Our client realized that assisted living and independent living were the most attractive areas, and that many companies currently were players in both segments. They began searching for prospects with both types of service in the geographic markets they desired, and they went on to make their first acquisition.

Market segmentation allows you to be more precise with your company searches, as well as reflecting the "how-to-eat-an-elephant" philosophy of growth through a series of smaller, targeted acquisitions.

Market Growth Rate

Along with market size, market growth rate is almost universally relevant as you seek to enter strong, expanding markets. Usually measured in percentages, a minimum growth rate is desired, along with a trend showing a stable or predictable pattern. This is the simplest indicator of healthy future demand, which in our model of external growth is normally the single most important determinant of success.

Major Players

Another factor you are likely to consider is the number and strength of major players. Is this a market dominated by one or two 800-pound gorillas, or is it reasonably divided among a number of leading contenders? The field always narrows at the top, but the question of how narrow gives an important indication of the competitive environment. For example, the aerospace industry is heavily consolidated at the top, while leadership of the more niche avionics market remains comparatively diverse, and such diversity can indicate greater scope for growth. People easily get the idea that a big market means big opportunities. But if that market is dominated by only a handful of players, it is difficult to create a strongly competitive presence unless you are introducing a truly disruptive technology. Of course, beneath the major players, there may be a much more even scattering of secondary companies in various support roles. Here you may well find a strong opportunity.

In a niche market, none of the major players is likely to be too large for you to consider as a partner, and this may provide the starting point for assembling your universe of companies to consider for acquisition. In any case, there is every reason to gather information about them as potential future competitors.

Customer Profile

The customer profile of a market is frequently an important consideration, including the question of how diverse or consolidated the customer base is. For instance, you may shy away from acquiring a prospect that serves the automobile manufacturing industry because it can supply only three major customers. The kind of customer a market serves is also significant: If your experience is exclusively business-to-business, you may think twice about buying a retailer. Your acquisition team may also wish to assess the switching costs for customers in the markets under review—a basic measure of customer loyalty.

Other Criteria

Other typical criteria used when evaluating markets include barriers to entry, technology requirements, and intellectual property issues. Again, though, you may have additional issues to consider that are exclusive to your company objectives or business environment.

THE MARKET CRITERIA MATRIX

Once you have decided on the criteria by which to choose a market, and the accompanying metrics to measure each individual criterion, you need a methodology for organizing and evaluating the information uncovered by your research. For this, we need the right tool: the Market Criteria Matrix.

The Market Criteria Matrix is a tool for helping you to rate markets in relation to your real-world priorities. There are three steps in establishing the Matrix. First, you identify your criteria. Next, you establish a metric for each one, so that you can make quantitative comparisons. Finally, you must weight your criteria.

We cannot overstate the importance of establishing metrics for each criterion. This is what saves your team discussions from becoming a fruitless conflict of subjective opinions. To take a typical example, you may decide that "positive company culture" is an important criterion. But how do you measure such a concept? One metric might be staff turnover. If people keep leaving, there's probably something amiss, while a company that wins long-term employee loyalty is likely to have a positive culture.

The last step—weighting the criteria—is easy to miss, because once you have your criteria and their associated metrics, it seems like a simple job to complete your ratings. However, this would neglect a crucial point. Not all your criteria are equally important to your growth objective. Simply listing them as if each has the same value distorts your picture and could lead to poor choices. It is essential to weight your criteria on a comparative basis, giving some more emphasis than others.

The process of weighting your criteria puts them into the right perspective. Perhaps market growth rate is paramount for your purposes, warranting, say, 30 percent of the total available score. At the same time, your team may conclude that barriers to entry are less significant and merit only 10 percent of the total market score. In that case, a market that wins high marks on "barriers to entry" may be set aside in favor of a market that does only moderately well in "market growth rate," because you give more weight to that all-important growth rate.

This step may draw your team into some lively disagreements about the relative significance of different criteria. As you resolve these points, you are preparing yourself for a later stage in the game, when you negotiate trade-offs. Knowing how to distinguish make-or-break requirements from merely desirable outcomes is a critical part of your acquisition planning.

When you have finished researching the possible markets, identified as best you can the metrics for each criterion, and completed your weighting, your A-Team should meet to score each market. Looking at the research, each team member gives a rating of 1 to 10 (with 10 being the highest) to indicate how well the market in question meets each criterion. Each rating is then multiplied by the previously assigned weight to achieve an adjusted score for that criterion. The individual criterion scores are added together to give a total score for the market. (See an example of a Market Criteria Matrix in Figure 5-2.)

To begin with, you are probably using this tool to assess broad market categories. Having conducted a weighted rating of each sector, you now have a relatively objective basis to decide which markets warrant in-depth research by examining more tightly niched segments.

For conducting comparisons at greater depth, I recommend what I call the Apples-to-Apples tool, as shown in Figure 5-3. This chart lists each market (or segment) you are examining on the horizontal axis, and the market criteria on the vertical axis.

CRITERIA	METRIC	WEIGHT	RATING	SCORE
BARRIERS TO ENTRY	- "Captive market" - Geographically defined - "Regulated" and/or government interaction - Intellectual property is required	**30%**		
CUSTOMERS	- Large customers - B2B preferred/wholesale; non-retail, non-consumer - Over $200M in revenue - Capital expenditure hurdles - Over $20M annually	**30%**		
GROWTH	- Stable and predictable - Sustainable - Not "fad" or "emerging" - Growing at 5% annually	**20%**		
COMPETITIVE ENVIRONMENT	- Fragmented competitor set - More than 10 - "Non-combative" competition (not price driven) - Service/"processing" preferred over manufacturing - Reputable players - Positive image, track record	**20%**		

Ratings are from 1-10
Score = weight x rating   **TOTAL** _____

Figure 5-2. An example of the Market Criteria Matrix.

When all your chosen market segments have been researched and evaluated, you can summarize your findings on the one page. I use a simple key to indicate which markets match up best with the criteria. If a market strongly meets the metrics for a particular criterion, I give it a check mark or I shade that box green. If only some of the metrics for a particular criterion are met, then the market gets a mark or is shaded yellow. If the market does not fit any of the metrics, then it is given an X or shaded red. This way, it is easy to see at a glance which markets are the most attractive and where to begin researching niches or individual companies. The more check marks or green areas for a market, the more attractive it is.

MARKET CRITERIA	MKT 1	MKT 2	MKT 3	MKT 4	MKT 5	MKT 6	MKT 7	MKT 8
GROWTH (25%) Stable, non-cyclical 15%/yr	✔	✔	✔	?	✔	✔	✔	X
SOLUTION (25%) Complementary and understandable product dynamics Sophisticated, high technology/need for unique product capabilities	?	?	?	?	?	?	?	✔
SIZE (20%) $50M-$100M Segment size	✔	✔	✔	✔	✔	✔	✔	✔
SEGMENT (15%) Global market "Under the radar of big players" Established, niche potential	✔	?	✔	?	✔	?	?	X
CUSTOMER CONCENTRATION (15%) At least 3 potential customers B2B, not B2C	?	?	?	?	✔	?	✔	✔
THE BOTTOM LINE Hold, Pursue or Pass	PURSUE	HOLD	PURSUE	PASS	PURSUE	HOLD	HOLD	PASS

Figure 5-3. An example of the Apples-to-Apples tool.

Note that although your focus at this stage is strictly markets, not companies, you are bound to come across individual companies of potential interest as acquisition partners. You would do well to have a system for recording this valuable information, to which you can return in the next stage of research. While you are studying markets, you can be implicitly building your list of potential prospects.

CONDUCTING EFFECTIVE RESEARCH

As I first mentioned in Chapter 3, thorough research has multiple benefits for the astute M&A operative. It sets you apart from other buyers by arming you with crucial information when approaching prospects. It also constitutes one of the early steps in the due diligence you would perform for any prospect. This is a vital consideration. The conventional concept of due diligence is a formal process that begins late in the buying process. With the Roadmap approach, your due diligence starts from Day One. Undertaking quality research early on protects you from costly surprises later and makes the formal vetting that is eventually required far smoother and less disruptive.

There is a significant difference between secondary and primary research, though both are important. Secondary research, where you draw from public sources such as the Internet and databases, is the easier of the two. When your focus is markets rather than individual companies, secondary research can reveal a wealth of information about market size, growth rates, supply chains, and other market dynamics. The U.S. government, Wall Street, and individual industry associations have plentiful market information publicly available that may be pertinent. (At the end of this book, you will find an introductory list of secondary research sources.)

Primary research requires that you talk one-on-one to active players in your selected markets. This process is invaluable for confirming or adjusting what you found through your secondary research, while capturing specific insights from those who deal with those markets every day.

Performing primary research successfully is an art. You are asking for people to spend time with you, answering your questions, with no obvious benefit to them. You must move quickly and be specific about your interests. Remember, you are not performing a survey but rather conducting an exploratory conversation. In the back of your mind, of course, you have a list of targeted issues about the market you are researching. However, you should avoid bombarding people with a series of questions. Rather, those questions should be mixed with comments and observations that you bring to the exchange. You can draw on your secondary research, which has given you a basic level of knowledge about the market, to build credibility with your sources. You can also play to your sources' egos, telling them that you understand that they are experts in the field and asking for their guidance. While you may occasionally run across someone who is unwilling to help (or is even rude), I have found that people generally like to talk about subjects on which they are considered knowledgeable.

Where do you find such experts? In any marketplace, there are three principal groups of players: suppliers, competitors, and customers. Each group may have quite different perspectives on the marketplace. Here are some of the general questions that I usually explore in my primary research for each group of players. Bear in mind that your question list should always be specific to your particular market criteria.

1. **Suppliers**
   - What kinds of products/services are you providing?
   - Who else is supplying this market?
   - Can you point to any current trends?
   - What do you see happening downstream?
   - Who are the leaders from a technology standpoint?
   - Where is current and/or future growth likely to come from?

2. **Competitors**
   - How do you segment the market?
   - What products/services are you providing to your marketplace?
   - Why do your customers buy from you?

- What are your customers' primary needs?
- What is driving growth in your industry?

3. **Customers**
- What are you buying, and why?
- What is the purchase process?
- What are your unmet needs?
- Will you continue to buy from your current supplier? Why or why not?
- Who are the other market players?
- Who is considered the best among your suppliers, and why?
- Are there any current trends that might affect your needs in the future?

Depending on the type of company you are approaching, you should turn to people in different functional areas to gain a good mix of perspectives. As a general rule, salespeople love to talk—it's their job! They can be a valuable source of information for much of what you are looking for. For more technical questions, you may need to consult operational managers. To gain financial insights, you want to approach a CFO or finance executive.

There are other industry experts that may be worth consulting as well. You may begin by contacting industry associations, which can be a valuable source for general trends and statistics. Journalists and editors from publications related to the market you are researching can also give a more detached perspective, while still throwing light on the market dynamics. Finally, if resources allow, you can often access a large pool of knowledge in a short amount of time by attending an industry trade show.

Whomever you talk to, it is important to bear in mind the difference between fact and opinion. When conducting primary research, it is always best to strive for facts to back up opinions, particularly since you have made a point of establishing your market criteria in measurable terms. One of your sources might throw out a comment like, "Information technology is one of the fastest growing segments in this market." While the observation may prove useful, it has far more value to you if you can find the numbers to back it up. A dependable source who says, "IT has been growing at 15 percent per year over the past five years and is projected to grow at 20 percent over the next three years" gives that opinion a more probable basis in fact.

ENGAGING A THIRD PARTY TO CONDUCT RESEARCH

In both your primary and secondary research, your overriding objective is to obtain as much reliable information as possible to complete the metrics you have set out for each criterion. There are a number of factors that can affect the thoroughness and reliability of the information you glean from your research.

One is resource allocation. The more time and manpower you can devote to it, the more thorough and reliable your research will be, particularly if you employ the techniques we have reviewed here.

Another factor is anonymity. This can present a tricky dilemma. On the one hand, you probably prefer to remain anonymous in your research activities so your competitors do not become wise to your acquisition strategy and preempt it. On the other hand, when you conduct primary research, there may be some sources who are unwilling to talk to you unless you reveal who you are and what company you are from.

Forthrightness and honesty are the best policies to follow when conducting research. Although you may be tempted to dissemble to maintain your anonymity, it can be damaging in the long run and destroy your credibility if you are found out. Word can travel fast in industry circles, where dishonesty with one company may damage your reputation with others in the industry—including a company you may be trying to acquire in the near future.

One means of avoiding the complications of limited resources and anonymity is to hire a third party to undertake your research. A consulting firm with experience in market research already knows where to look for key information—both secondary and primary—particularly if the firm specializes in acquisition projects. The firm's personnel can turn to resources they have used in the past and ask the right questions in order to get the information you need. Third parties do not have to reveal your company name while doing research, keeping your company anonymous until it is advantageous to reveal it. They never have to be dishonest, since they can reveal only basic information you authorize and politely decline if asked for more. Sources generally understand and respect this situation, and it is rarely detrimental to research efforts.

SHIFTING FOCUS FROM MARKETS TO PROSPECTS

As we have seen, thorough market research usually requires multiple rounds—a broad sweep of macro markets and then an incremental zeroing in on specific segments and, possibly, sub-segments. As you progress through the research process, you may find yourself challenged to refine and change your market criteria based on information you discover. For example, you might find a market growth rate of 10 percent simply unrealistic in the face of current statistics, and you may have to lower the bar to, say, 5 percent. This kind of adjustment is healthy and keeps the research process dynamic and rooted in reality.

With primary and secondary research complete, your A-Team is positioned to make an informed decision about which market to focus on in the search for target acquisitions. This decision should be based on the agreed criteria, weighted by importance, and as far as possible expressed in measurable form. By now, you have already brought to the acquisition process a far higher level of system and objectivity than is common in the world of M&A. It is this "engineered" approach to acquisition that can place your project in the minority of truly successful acquisitions.

PREPARING FOR THE NEXT STAGE

If you have followed the Roadmap to this point, you have established your business objectives, your pathway to growth, and your single reason for making an acquisition. You have also assembled your acquisition team and chosen the precise market where you will search for an acquisition partner. Now we enter the second stage, *Build the Relationships*, as you venture out to find prospects and make contact with companies that you may one day acquire. This stage presents a new set of challenges and opportunities. Your first step is to identify the most promising not-for-sale companies that match your one reason to buy.

PART 2

BUILD THE RELATIONSHIPS

CHAPTER 6

THE PROSPECT FUNNEL

WE ARE READY TO BEGIN the second stage of the Roadmap process for acquisition: *Build the Relationships*. Now that you've mapped out your overall strategy and identified your target markets, you can go in search of individual acquisition prospects. A word of warning here: You are shifting from the relative comfort of abstract strategy to dealing with real companies and real people. At this point, I have noticed that acquisition teams tend to become much more emotionally involved—sometimes to the detriment of the process. The solution as always is a strong system, because only a system enables you to take the emotion out of your decision making. To be clear, I am not saying that the pursuit of prospects should be undertaken without a measure of excitement or passion. To "take the emotion out" means to conduct your search using a structured process and objective tools, and returning to those tools at the key decision points.

The basis of the system we will be using is what I call the Prospect Funnel. Anyone familiar with the traditional sales funnel will recognize the principle at play here: a progressive narrowing of focus from the many to the few. This is achieved by grounding all your activities in clearly defined criteria. In what follows, I introduce some critical guidelines for the successful investigation of individual companies. I also present some of the key tools my team uses to help our clients compare and contrast choices. For you, the end result will be a short, organized list of companies with whom you can initiate negotiations, confident that they are the most appropriate candidates for a successful acquisition.

WHY A FUNNEL?

I have frequently been approached by clients after a deal suddenly fell through—a deal they had been working on for months or even years. I recall a manufacturer of agricultural equipment that was convinced from the start that they had found the "Holy Grail" of acquisition targets. They believed this prospect was the perfect fit for their external growth needs. They cast aside all other candidates and poured all their energy into the pursuit of this one company. After months of positive negotiations, the prospect abruptly got cold feet and backed out. The owner decided he wasn't ready to sell a business that had been in family hands for multiple generations. The agricultural equipment manufacturer was left to start the entire acquisition process over.

The lesson is clear: Have one reason for making an acquisition, but have many viable prospects. Don't just have a Plan B. Have a Plan C, a Plan D, and so on. Create a funnel and fill it with likely prospects. This approach yields many benefits. The concept of the Prospect Funnel is that you begin by considering a broad sweep of companies. It could be dozens or even hundreds. Gradually, you filter this list through your prospect criteria, eliminating weaker candidates step-by-step. At each stage, as you move down the funnel, your research becomes more detailed and your analysis more exacting. Finally, you identify a handful worth engaging personally, and from these you select the company or companies with whom you initiate negotiations for a purchase (see Figure 6-1).

Prospects that survive to the narrower selection may be set aside

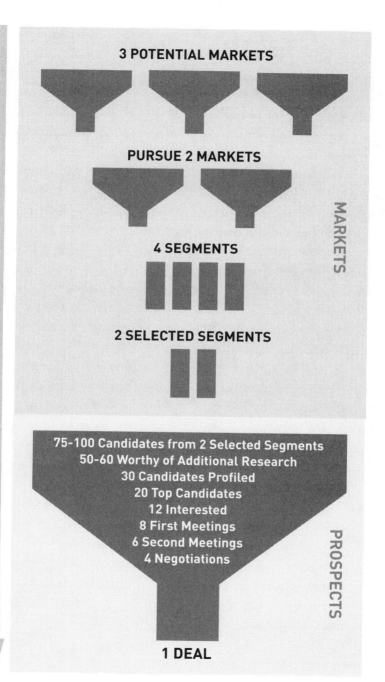

Figure 6-1. The Prospect Funnel.

but are never discarded. Rather, they are the backups for when things go wrong with your initial preference—which is almost inevitable. Like the agricultural equipment manufacturer mentioned above, you may find yourself falling in love with a prospect, but they back out at the last minute. Worse yet, you could "dance" with a prospect throughout the entire process, only to see a rival swoop in and leave with them at the end of the night.

Having multiple prospects actually accelerates the acquisition process. The head of a specialty chemical company once hired us to help with negotiations with a target he was interested in. It turned out he had been in discussions with this prospect for two years, but they were no closer to finalizing the deal. Once my firm was engaged, my first question was, "Who else are you in discussions with?" The client stared back at me with a deer-in-the-headlights look and responded, "What do you mean? We haven't closed this deal yet." Realizing that all his eggs were in one basket, I saw that our first task was to develop a pipeline of other prospect companies. Within sixty days, we were in negotiations with three other businesses. This allowed my client to assess the comparative value of the original company he had been talking to. It also gave more confidence to the negotiations, which finally led to an acquisition agreement.

So, in the first place, the Prospect Funnel is an insurance policy: Your acquisition process can continue unhindered if there is a breakdown with a favored prospect. There are other benefits, though. Having several well-researched prospects gives you a sound basis for comparison as you gather more and more information on your priority targets. Finally, the funnel approach enables you to tee up for the next acquisition the moment the first purchase is complete, and in rare circumstances, it allows you to consider buying multiple companies at the same time.

ESTABLISHING PROSPECT CRITERIA

How do you initiate your Prospect Funnel? There are no surprises here: The first step is to establish your prospect criteria. As with market criteria, your prospect criteria need to be rooted in your one reason for acquisition, which in turn is based on your larger business strategy.

I recommend that when you sit down with your A-Team to assemble your search criteria, you begin by defining an "ideal prospect." If you could have your wish fulfilled for a dream prospect, what would that company look like? Figure 6-2, the Prospect Criteria Matrix, lists some common parameters to help you fill out the profile. Notice that for each criterion, there is space for you to indicate the metrics that would give objectivity to your ratings.

Drawing on your completed Prospect Criteria Matrix, write up your description of the "perfect" acquisition company. The criteria and metrics should describe the ideal candidate so actual companies can be compared for objective evaluation and prioritization.

While reality is unlikely ever to match this perfect picture, the exercise should yield a very effective list of criteria for your search.

The same rules we discussed for creating market criteria apply to your prospect criteria. You still want to limit the criteria to no more than six, focusing first on strategic aspects. Again, you need to establish metrics to ensure that your criteria are measurable. This

OCKOUT FACTORS: Screening Filter)	1 _____	2 _____	
CRITERIA	**METRIC**		**WEIGHT**
OWNERSHIP/MGMT.			
CUSTOMER			
FINANCIAL			
PRODUCTS			
MARKETS			

Figure 6-2. The Prospect Criteria Matrix.

may be more difficult with a parameter such as "management expe-rience," but you still need a way to measure it. Here, your metric could be "executive team in place for at least five years."

As with your market criteria, you should weight the importance of the prospect criteria, apportioning a certain percentage to each criterion for a total of 100 percent. As your research proceeds, you and your A-Team should use the Prospect Criteria Matrix to priori-tize prospects that warrant more research and resources. You should score prospects on how well they match each criterion on a 1 to 10 scale, multiply that by the criterion's weight, then add the weighted scores together to arrive at a total score for that prospect. The higher the score, the further the prospect moves into the funnel.

The Prospect Criteria Matrix gives your acquisition team an opportunity to discuss what they like and dislike about a prospect. It is to be expected that members of the A-Team may disagree on their criteria scores for a particular prospect. Disagreement adds clarity to the process as issues are put on the table and healthy dis-cussion ensues. It also helps sharpen the distinctions between com-panies in your Prospect Funnel.

When establishing your criteria for researching individual com-panies, as opposed to entire markets, you have to be realistic about the availability of information. Any difficulties you faced eliciting information during your market research are likely to be amplified when it comes to company research. Later in the chapter, I'll reveal my tactics for extracting as much information as possible for com-pany research. In terms of criteria, though, beware of establishing metrics that depend on confidential, internal data from your pro-spective companies. You are unlikely to get it during the initial research phase.

THE VALUE OF OBJECTIVITY

Using objective criteria can help with what, in my firm, we call "brother-in-law" companies. These are companies that a CEO believes are a great deal because she has access to a special information source (such as a brother-in-law inside the organization). When we research companies like this, we often find that they do not smell as sweet as our client believes. By applying rigorous and systematic research to the prospect criteria, we are able to demonstrate that the juicy information may not indicate such a great fit.

The opposite has also happened. The CEO of a financial services client had already heard of a company we found through our independent research and had formed a negative impression of it. Apparently, the prospect was "too small" and "mom-and-popish." It turned out that the CEO had not had contact with the company in question for ten years. In the meantime, it had grown to be quite a robust corporation. Once filtered through the prospect criteria, it moved to the top of the prospect list.

Using the Prospect Criteria Matrix to assess "brother-in-law companies" enables your acquisition team to have a logical dialogue with the CEO about the merits of the prospect. I often jokingly ask, "How do you publicly tell a CEO that this is a dumb idea? . . . You can do it once but not twice!" Using an objective tool allows you to communicate your doubts and keep your job.

The lesson is clear: Always do your research and use your criteria to get an *objective* view of any market or prospect.

DETERMINING THE COMPANY DNA

Here we must introduce a crucial principle of prospect research. Right from the beginning, even when you are dealing with secondary sources, you should be looking for more than hard data to complete the metrics in your prospect criteria. You should also be trying to figure out the "company DNA." As stated in Chapter 1, what I mean here is the culture of the company—its heart and soul. Be aware that this usually takes painstaking inquiry. I have had clients say to me that they can figure out a company's culture by sitting down and looking the CEO in the eye. I usually respond, "OK, what part of the eyeball do you look at to find culture?" I am not trying to be flippant but rather to point out that a company's culture is complex, like biological DNA, and it cannot be determined simply through one meeting with a CEO.

To explore a company's culture, I like to start with a glance at the company website to see what (or whom) they are emphasizing and what descriptive words they are using. As you read about a company, whether on their website or in articles you uncover, look beyond products and sales figures to see how (or if) they engage with their employees, their community, and their overall business environment. As far as possible, you want to gain multiple perspectives from inside and outside. Is the company seen as a good place to work? Has it won the respect of suppliers and even competitors? Is it perceived locally as a good corporate citizen? As you move forward in the acquisition process and start to talk to people, you will naturally get a more in-depth feel of the company DNA.

CASTING A WIDE NET

Once you and your A-Team determine your prospect criteria, you can start finding companies to fill the funnel and rate them according to the criteria. Your goal is to cast a net far, wide, and deep in order to establish the largest possible pool of initial candidates in your target market. At this early stage, you want to avoid unintentionally excluding any viable companies. Needless to say, the primary focus is on not-for-sale companies, a far bigger population than the minority of businesses actively seeking a buyer.

Your initial prospect list usually comes from a few different sources. First, you can include the companies you uncovered during your market research. In Chapter 5, I recommended you make note of any promising companies you came across during your market research. This stage is where the discipline pays off.

Second, you should have a discussion with your A-Team about significant players in the market(s) you have chosen. Since your team members are drawn from different departments in your company, they may have encountered a variety of interesting companies. Team members should in turn consult other employees for their input. Because of the nature of their work, sales and marketing personnel in particular are often familiar with a wide range of companies.

Once you have started your list from these sources, you begin to build on it. I like to expand the list based on three parameters: products, technologies, and customers. For example, you may have discovered during market research a company that produces a certain type of widget. By searching for other companies that specialize in equivalent widgets, you can enlarge your prospect pool. Likewise, when you use technology to expand the list, you might focus on a particular manufacturing process. As for customers, I would be looking at who else is selling to similar customers in your selected market segments. Think back to the seafood company I discussed in Chapter 3 that wanted to supplement its offerings with value-added products. When we put together its initial prospect list, we looked at typical customers for value-added seafood products and found out which companies were currently serving those customers. We discovered that companies selling to supermarkets, to distributors like Sysco, or to governments (for schools and jails) were all potential acquisition candidates, and then we made the initial list.

GATHERING SECONDARY RESEARCH

So, how do you find more companies to fill the top of the funnel and place on your initial prospect list? The answer is secondary research: the careful sifting through of publicly available data. Just as with secondary market research, your search for prospects begins with using the Internet, databases, and other public sources. Simply plugging keywords or company names into search engines like Google or Yahoo! can get you started building your top-level prospect list.

More efficient than search engines, though, are business databases such as OneSource or LexisNexis. In addition to company names, they provide information like revenue estimates and executive lists, as well as news articles and industry data. This can be enough information for you to begin completing the metrics for your prospect criteria. Another advantage of these databases is that they often list "similar" companies, immediately expanding your pool.

Other key secondary sources are company websites and annual reports. Websites can offer a trove of information, including product lines, manufacturing capabilities, and pricing information. At the same time, you have to allow for bias when looking at a company website, because the company is naturally trying to portray itself in the best light possible. The same caveat applies to annual reports. They can offer insight into strategy and give detailed financials, but they can also be pervaded by spin.

CONDUCTING PRIMARY RESEARCH: THE INFORMATION DANCE

Secondary research can bring you through your first couple of phases of prospect screening and prioritization, but as you move further down the funnel and narrow your search, you need more precise tools.

To really get to know a company, you must do primary research. This involves getting on the phone and talking to people who deal with the company on a regular basis, and eventually to the principals themselves. As in the market research phase, I recommend "triangulating" the process to gain multiple perspectives. In this case, triangulating involves speaking to suppliers, competitors, and customers of the prospect. Once you have a sense of what people on the outside are saying, you want to speak directly to the company owners.

Primary prospect research often requires a defter handling of phone conversations than market research. This is what I call "the information dance." Through years of experience, I have developed some general guidelines on how best to perform the dance—in other words, how to conduct yourself when eliciting information about a specific company.

◆ **Be prepared with a plan and appropriate contacts.** Before you dial, know what information you are trying to uncover and whom you can best get it from. If you are discussing a technology, the engineering department is probably your best starting point. Salespeople are usually valuable for researching a company's reputation. In addition, when a source drops a name, make note of it and contact that person next.

◆ **Be informed about the prospect and the market.** Through your market research and secondary prospect research, you should have obtained a baseline of information that gives you credibility when speaking to a source. You may want to discuss the prospect company in the context of industry trends, so you need to know what those trends are. Reread your market and prospect information before picking up the phone.

◆ **Be honest.** As with market research, honesty in prospect research is always the best policy. This doesn't mean that you need to reveal your entire strategic plan to a stranger on the phone. It means don't lie. You can reveal as little or as much information as you feel comfortable with, but understand that your own disclosures may not be enough to persuade the other person to reveal the data you seek.

◆ **Be creative.** When discussing a company, you often want to start off slow before zeroing in on specific information. You can even ask questions you already know the answers to in order to get the conversation rolling, and then move on to more significant areas. You may already know the company's main products, but asking that question can be a setup for asking how those products compare to others in the market. You need to gain the trust of your source before extracting the gritty details of a company.

→ **Be persistent, but not annoying.** Leaving messages is fine, and if you don't get a call back, wait a few days and then try again. There is no need to call every day or multiple times in a day. If there is no reply after the first few messages, move on to another source. Also, when someone you are interviewing doesn't have a piece of information you are seeking, politely ask who in his company might, and when you are done, ask to be transferred to pick up those nuggets.

→ **Be realistic, and prepare for rejection.** Some people are so skeptical of your motives that they simply won't want to talk to you. Others become uncomfortable if you ask them to reveal too much information. You may hear the word "proprietary" over and over. Don't let this get you down. Just move on to the next source.

To make a success of your primary market research, you must be nimble and ready to adjust your line of questioning when you stumble. Remember, you are not conducting an interrogation but holding a conversation. To succeed with the information dance, you must be prepared to move with artistry.

One important skill is to match your expectations to the stage of the dance. With a private company, you shouldn't expect to get a copy of last year's financials the first time you call! In the absence of exact numbers, you have to make guesses based on the best information you do have. Company information takes the form of a continuum. You start off with the more general, public information you have from secondary research, and as you move through primary research, meetings, and negotiations, you learn more and more about your prospect.

The information dance is inherently difficult, but you do have the option of hiring a dance master to perform the steps for you. There are obvious advantages to enrolling a qualified third-party team to conduct your primary prospect research. The team members' experience allows them to ask the right questions immediately with a minimal learning curve. They have the ability to cut through the veneer salespeople or executives sometimes put up, eliciting the information that is actually important. They know the right tone to use with sources and the best people to contact for a given piece of data. Perhaps most important, they can protect your anonymity until you decide the time is right to reveal yourself.

TOOLS THAT ORGANIZE AND PRIORITIZE

As you gather an increasing volume of information about a prospect, you need to organize it so that the key elements are easily accessible. I suggest using a Prospect Profile. This is a document that lists basic company information (e.g., address, website, CEO), followed by your detailed research data listed in bullet form and sorted to match your prospect criteria. You can also include pictures of key products, quotes from interviews, information on the company's culture, and anything else you believe is particularly relevant about a prospect. The profile grows over time as you uncover more information.

Your Prospect Profiles serve as the basis for evaluating each prospect using your predefined criteria. This prioritization process happens repeatedly during the prospect research and selection phase. Once you have your initial list of companies and have conducted preliminary secondary research on them, you can rank them to decide which of them merit in-depth secondary research. This ranking and narrowing should continue throughout the research phase, and throughout the acquisition process as a whole, as you continually reprioritize your prospect list to decide where best to devote your resources.

I also suggest you use my Prospect Tracker tool (see Figure 6-3). This shows where you are in the acquisition process with each prospect company.

Prospects are listed on the vertical axis in the "Company" column, and the different phases of the acquisition process are shown

STATUS	COMPANY	ID & SCREEN	PROFILE & OWNER CONTACT	1st VISIT	MEETINGS/ DUE DILIGENCE	NEGOTIATIONS	NOTES
PURSUE	Acme Corp.	✔	✔	✔	✔	✔	Ongoing interest, need board approval
PURSUE	XTZ Inc.	✔	✔	✔	✔		Ongoing interest, return visit planned
PURSUE	ESP Ltd.	✔	✔	✔	✔		Ongoing interest, MOU signed
PURSUE	Standard Inc.	✔	✔				Ongoing interest, 1st visit planned
PURSUE	Jones Corp.	✔	✔				Ongoing interest, need to schedule 1st visit
HOLD	B&E Corp. Orange Ltd.	✔	✔				Interested but not good timing, call in 6 months
PASS	20+ Others	✔	✔				Not interested at this time

Figure 6-3. An example of the Prospect Tracker tool.

on the horizontal axis. These include secondary research (identification and screening), primary research (profiling), owner contacts, meetings (including due diligence), and negotiations. As you move from one phase to the next—say, from primary research to contacting the owner—you check the appropriate box for that prospect (for instance, "Owner Contact"). Now you have a one-glance document to determine where you are in the acquisition process with each prospect. When you are dealing with hundreds of companies, this tool becomes an essential resource for keeping track of your progress with each of them.

EARLY DUE DILIGENCE

Many people mistakenly see due diligence as a formal process of checking documents toward the end of the acquisition process. In reality, due diligence embraces every form of research that provides insight on a target company, and it should begin early. Prospect research is a critical form of due diligence, and if conducted properly, it makes the later stages far easier to complete. You are uncovering information about a company in order to determine if you want to move forward in the acquisition process. While you are not being handed the accounting ledgers for review, you are gaining an early glimpse of how the company operates and how it is perceived in the marketplace. By the time you conduct your formal investigations, you should be in a position to confirm in detail the company profile you have already developed.

Thorough prospect research and selection leads directly to the next phase of the acquisition process: owner contacts. Research helps you determine which owners you want to contact out of the universe of companies you have considered. More than that, your acquaintance with the company and its business environment helps you establish credibility once you get that owner on the phone. The better informed you are, the more effectively you can build a relationship that may lead to eventual union.

CHAPTER 7

MAKING THE
FIRST CONTACT

YOU HAVE REACHED A critical moment in the Roadmap process. Having identified the target companies you would like to consider acquiring, you are ready to make contact with the owners. The first connection is a decisive step. Handled correctly, it can initiate a positive relationship that may eventually lead to union. Handled poorly, that one phone call can terminate your opportunity to buy.

In this chapter, after discussing some important considerations, we begin our focus on making the first contact with owners by reviewing your preparations—deciding whom to contact and who does the contacting. Next, we consider motivations—understanding why a particular owner might want to sell, and how this insight can be used to your advantage. Finally, I walk you through that all-important first call—including what to say and how to respond when the owner inevitably says "no."

SOME CRITICAL CONSIDERATIONS

Prior to your initial contact with owners of companies that look appealing for acquisition, there are a few crucial considerations.

Assuming your focus is not-for-sale, private companies, you are dealing with a paradox. On the one hand, the company's owner is not actively looking to sell, and she therefore may be expected to respond negatively to any overtures. On the other hand, we have established an inviolable law of M&A: Every company is for sale for the right equation. By simultaneously grasping each side of this paradox, you can prepare for a successful approach.

Obviously, no one is going to sell her company to a complete stranger over the phone. So the purpose of your initial call is *not* to buy the company. Your purpose is to start a dialogue. More precisely, the only outcome you need from that first call is a follow-up call or a face-to-face meeting. The question is: What kind of relationship are you initiating, and what might motivate the owner to continue the conversation?

To answer this, let's look again at our core assumption. We know there is an equation for which the owner will sell. But we don't know what that equation is—and the owner may not either! What needs to happen at the outset of the relationship is that a vision begins to form, in your mind as well as the owner's. It's a vision of a possible fusion of two companies. It's a vision of successful synergies and profitable growth. It's a strategic vision more than a financial one. At this stage, you are not approaching the owner with a checkbook but with a plan.

So now a new question arises: How do you give credibility to your vision? You can hardly start fleshing out a detailed acquisition plan—remember, you don't yet know the owner's equation. You create credibility by demonstrating the depth of your knowledge. This is where all that exhaustive market and company research comes in. Sometimes the biggest return on your investment in research appears in the first few moments on the phone with an owner. Your understanding of the company's history, strengths, and business environment makes a lasting impression. Your appreciation for the owner's role in that story establishes a personal link.

This leads to one further consideration that follows from the approach we have outlined here. In the initial contact, you must avoid what I call "the price trap." You should not touch the question of how much you are willing to pay. There are two reasons for this. First, it is far too early in the process to know what price range is appropriate. Much more important, any mention of price pushes the conversation into a binary yes-or-no corner. As I have stressed, every company is for sale for the right *equation*—of which price is only one component. It is quite likely the owner has been approached before to sell the company and has refused a handsome cash offer. Many factors may be more important to the owner, as we'll see later in this chapter when we explore buyer psychology. So even if the other party raises the question of price early on, you want to steer the conversation back to the strategic benefits of a possible deal.

The idea that price is not always the dominant consideration may seem counterintuitive, so let me give you an example from my own practice. A large foreign manufacturer of medical appliances with about $1 billion in revenue approached me looking to extend their global reach by acquiring a U.S.-based manufacturer in the $80 million to $100 million range. We helped them find the optimum prospect and placed the initial call. Because of our research, we astonished the owners with our knowledge of their business and industry. We began unfolding a strategic vision for the union of the two companies, and the prospect became receptive to the idea of selling. Then it turned out that the owners had just hired a firm to start the auction process to sell the company. Unfortunately, it was too late to stop the auction. Nevertheless, my client continued negotiations, and we placed our own bid into the auction. After a few rounds, we won the deal. Now here is the moral of the story. We found out later that our bid was *lower* than some of the other bids. So why did my client win the auction? The owners were so impressed by our knowledge of the industry and our strategic growth plan for the future that they preferred our client over other suitors offering more cash. The right equation trumped the better price.

CONTACT STRATEGY

Before people from your company begin to speak to owners, you need to determine a contact strategy based around three key points: whom you are contacting from the prospect's organization, who is making the contact on behalf of your organization, and the method of approach.

Assuming your research has brought you to the point of initiating a connection, you should have an idea of whom to call first at the prospect company. Needless to say, this can be more complicated than simply asking to speak with "the owner." Companies can have multiple owners or an owner who is only passively involved in the business. You may need to make multiple contacts and carry on separate dialogues with several different people in the same target company.

As to who should be making the first contact, it may seem intuitive that when contacting an owner, the best person in your organization to make the call is your own CEO, who may even know the individual in question. In Chapter 4, I laid out a limited role for the CEO in the acquisition process, with carefully defined responsibilities. In this spirit, I caution against the CEO being the one to first make contact with an owner. Having a preexisting relationship with an owner can actually create an awkward situation as you start to ask probing questions about the target company from a buyer's point of view.

Instead, it's often a wise idea to have your adviser make the initial contact. Here's one instance where the use of a third party makes particular sense. An outside consultant can maintain your anonymity at this exploratory stage, interviewing owners to gauge their attitudes toward a potential partnership. If, after these initial calls, you decide that you do not want to continue with a particular company, they will be none the wiser. If you do wish to proceed, you can then reveal yourself on your terms.

Third-party experts can also bring their years of experience in contacting owners and discovering their hot buttons. It takes considerable skill to quickly catch an owner's interest, extend the conversation, and identify the underlying issues. So when you have only one chance to make a good first impression, it helps to have someone at your side who has been in that situation many times before. The probing questions that may cause an awkward situation between CEOs are expected from third parties, and prospects are more likely to open up to them. Just as you may not tell all of your health problems to your friends, you would have no problem explaining them to a doctor—an outside expert.

You may have noticed that in discussing the initial contact, I refer to making a phone call. This may seem unremarkable, but I have found that the idea of contacting owners by phone is actually somewhat unusual. I estimate that 85 percent of third-party advisers, including investment bankers, first contact a prospect by letter. While this option may be less costly in time, you get what you pay for. With a letter, you have no way of knowing how the owner immediately reacted or even if the letter was actually read. A phone call allows you to respond instantly to any questions or concerns, as well as to ramp up excitement by laying out your vision tailored to that specific company.

BUYER PSYCHOLOGY 101

The first conversation with a prospect should only be exploratory and focused on the broadest vision. Nevertheless, this call actually opens the negotiation process. What is said here becomes part of the give-and-take of later, more direct deal making. As with any negotiation, the key to success is understanding the other party's frame of mind.

Before you dial, you need to make some educated guesses about the person on the other end of the line, drawing on your company research. What you surmise should guide your approach. You need to talk to the fourth-generation owner of a family business quite differently from how you speak with the manager of a private equity fund who has held a company for only a couple of years. Age can also have an effect on how you make your approach. Think back to the story I shared in the introduction. Anthony, the company owner, had no financial need to continue working, but he did so every day because it was what he enjoyed most. For some older owners, coming into the office is fun, and they want to make sure their life's work is in good hands. Younger owners may be less invested, either emotionally or financially. Different owners may also have different pressures on them from family or the community. Take careful note if a number of family members are employed or if you have found newspaper articles detailing community involvements such as participation in local charities or business organizations.

All of these factors—history, age, family, community—shape an owner's mindset and affect his initial response to your approach. You may or may not refer explicitly to such issues in the first call, but you can be assured they will surface as negotiations move forward. The point is to hold them in mind so you find the right tone and language to capture the owner's interest.

While many concerns will be unique to the particular owner you are speaking to, there is one universal principle that governs the courtship of any prospective acquisition: An inherent asymmetry puts the buyer and seller on different planes. You can buy companies over and over again, but the owner can sell his company only once. Though you may be taking significant risks with making an acquisition—financially, strategically, perhaps personally—nevertheless, there is likely to be far more at stake for the owner. If you fail at this purchase, you can always attempt another. But if the owner messes up the sale, a lifetime's work may be lost. This asymmetry understandably puts sellers in a position where they are both cautious and skeptical.

THE OWNER'S HOT BUTTONS

Despite all their natural anxieties, owners do sell their businesses for a variety of reasons. It is essential that you have a general grasp of likely motivations because the underlying driver may not appear at once. One common reason owners sell is to "take some chips off the table." They may have much of their net worth invested in the business, and selling could give them a degree of security moving forward. In another instance, owners may be seeking funds for expansion, so they sell part of the business in order to meet their capital needs. The company (or the owner) may be in financial trouble, and selling is a way out. While you may be justifiably wary of a situation like this, it is not a reason to automatically reject a prospect. There may be other qualities that make the deal attractive, and a change in ownership and management can often rectify financial difficulties.

Owners frequently sell because they see bigger opportunities for their company as part of a larger organization. They may recognize selling as a way to tap the value of their ideas or capture market opportunities. In this case, they usually want to stay on after the deal is done. Although they will undoubtedly lose some control, this is offset by the opportunity of growth for their company through access to new markets or customers.

As you engage owners in conversation, you need to listen for factors that might prompt them to sell. These factors are the owners' "hot buttons." They are, in effect, the nonmonetary part of the equation that you are trying to put together. Are you talking to an older owner in estate-planning mode, the proud inheritor of a multigenerational family concern, or to an upstart young entrepreneur? Because the right equation for each prospect is different, the appropriate angle of attack must be adopted from the start.

You may have noticed that I always refer to making contact with the *owner*—not "management" or "stakeholders" or "key people." I believe it is vital that you start at the top with the very first conversation. The owner is the one who has the final say on whether to sell or not, so this is the person you must hook with your vision of partnership. When it comes to something as crucial as selling all or part of the company, only the owner has the real power to move the process on to the next stage.

THE ART OF THE PHONE

Everything we have explored so far is contingent on your success in keeping the owner on the phone long enough to start a fruitful conversation. That requires skill on your part. The rest of this chapter is dedicated to techniques for getting you in touch with the owner, staying on the phone, and scheduling another call or meeting.

Despite the popular cliché, attitude isn't everything, though it counts for a great deal in your initial approach to not-for-sale owners. Going into the first call, you need to show confidence and conviction. This confidence is instilled by all of your preparation through market and prospect research. You know the company and you know the industry it is in. You also know why this company would be a good strategic fit and why an acquisition would be mutually beneficial. Your job is to entice the owner with a compelling vision of the future. In other words, although ostensibly you are the buyer, your true role at this stage is to become a salesperson, promoting the strategic opportunity and whetting the owner's appetite for the exciting outcomes of combining the two companies.

The Call Structure

It may take some persistence to get owners on the phone in the first place, but once you do, I recommend a three-step process for capturing their interest and keeping them engaged.

First, you must establish credibility. As I've mentioned, you are probably not the first one to approach the owner about selling her company. Within the first minute of the call, you must impress her with your knowledge of the business. Once she senses that you have put in the time and effort to learn about her company, you will be set apart as someone with credibility.

Then, you need to draw the owner into a two-way conversation. Briefly outline your understanding of the company and why you think the combination of the two companies would be a good strategic fit. Ask her, given this rationale, if she could see value in a union—even on a provisional basis. If she says "no," keep the conversation going by asking "Why not?" This is where you need to listen most actively and be ready to respond in a way that shows appreciation for the other person's perspective. As you begin to uncover the owner's concerns (her hot buttons), you can start identifying possible variables in the sale equation. Throughout this conversation, it pays to be nimble and to avoid yes-or-no questions. You may have a script of questions you want to get answers to, but it rarely happens that you get all the answers on the first call. You are not conducting a survey. You are initiating a friendly discussion about growth strategy.

Finally, you want to establish a next step. Whether it's another phone call or a date for a meeting, you can show the owner that you are serious and will take the time to make sure things are done in a way that is beneficial to all parties involved. Remember, the ultimate goal for your first call is to open the door for another conversation.

LEARN TO LOVE "NO"

I have rarely found an owner who, when asked if he would consider selling his business, immediately says, "Yes, I want to sell, and I want to sell now." If you did actually get an immediate yes, this might well indicate weakness on the part of the prospect. Sometimes, I do hear, "Everything is for sale, except the wife and kids, for the right price." Most often, though, the responses you are most likely to hear are "probably not," "not right now," or flat out "no, thanks." When this happens, you may be tempted to give up and move to the next prospect. That would be a huge mistake. In fact, you should embrace every rejection, because if you listen carefully to the reasons, they can lead you to the hidden equation for which the owner will, in fact, sell. In reality, you haven't been rejected at all. For company owners, "no" is a knee-jerk response. It's simply a lot easier for them to say "no" than "yes." All it means is: Your strategic vision doesn't yet make sense.

My firm often takes the role of making the first approach to a target company on behalf of a client. A case in point was for a welding equipment manufacturer that wanted to make a strategic purchase of a significant competitor. We called the owner of the competitor, at first not disclosing our client's name. As expected, when we floated the idea of a purchase, the owner immediately said, "No." In fact, he went even further to say, "If your client is Company X, there is no way I would ever sell to them." Our client was, in fact, that very same Company X. Instead of retreating, we disclosed the name and probed the owner to discover the source of his aversion. As we came to understand his issues, we began to address them and eventually put together the precise equation that would encourage him to sell. We followed through on due diligence and negotiations until we successfully concluded the acquisition—from a man who had said he would *never* sell his company to our client.

There are a number of lessons to draw from this one brief case. First, "no" does not necessarily mean "no." It means "solve my problem." Second, what closes the deal is not the right price but the right equation. And third, an intermediary can sometimes initiate a relationship that would be barred to you from the start.

Timing is often a key aspect of the equation, and it is worth staying in contact with a prospect who has turned you down, especially if the person says the timing isn't right. I recommend communicating at least quarterly after the initial contact and getting together once a year to keep in touch.

FROM COURTING TO DATING

In this chapter, we've seen the importance of the first call and we've reviewed a methodology that ensures that you take advantage of the unique opportunity this initial contact represents. Preparation is key: You need to have a solid understanding of the business and of the market it is in, as well as of the owner's possible motivations for selling. You should always go straight to the top and connect directly with the owner or owners. As for the conversation itself, the key is unfolding an enticing vision and not being discouraged by the first, second, or even third "no."

Your success at this stage is contingent on your faith in the principle that every company is for sale for the right equation. Once you fully own that belief, your task becomes one of figuring out that equation through additional contact, whether through meetings or phone calls. If you keep connecting with the prospect, at some point down the road the complete equation will reveal itself. At that point, you can decide whether the deal is right for *you*. Now the tables have turned to the buyer's advantage, and it becomes your call whether to say "yes" or "no."

In the next chapter, we explore how best to plan and execute a face-to-face meeting between buyer and seller. You've started the courtship process. Now it's time for the first date.

CHAPTER 8

FACE-TO-FACE
WITH OPPORTUNITY

YOU ARE NOW READY to meet the owner of your prospective purchase face-to-face. If the primary outcome of your first phone call was to establish credibility, your goal now is to create trust between the two parties. Trust means far more than exchanging nondisclosure agreements. It also involves establishing a rapport between buyer and seller, which is always better accomplished in person. So this encounter comes at a crucial point in the developing relationship between you and your prospect. It's like a first date, and you want to put your best foot forward.

In this chapter, we begin by considering the logistics of the first visit—who should go, what to send beforehand, and how to give the owner the role of host. Once those details are taken care of, we look at how to prepare for the meeting in collaboration with your A-Team. Finally, we walk through a typical visit and, assuming there is mutual interest, discuss how to set up a second "date."

As my clients plan the initial meeting, I always remind them that they are not shopping for a used car. People's livelihood is on the table, and perhaps their whole sense of personal identity. I have previously described the inherent asymmetry of "buy often, sell once."

As you approach your first meeting, remember that you may be looking to purchase a business that has been in a family for generations. Understanding the owner's situation and the company history is the key to creating trust. By adopting an attitude of respect and listening carefully to what sellers have to say, you can make them more comfortable with the idea of letting go of all or part of their business.

BEFORE YOU GO

The role of salesperson that you undertook during your initial phone contacts continues through your first meeting. Even though you are the buyer, you are really trying to sell the vision of a union between two companies with all the resultant benefits and synergies. Preparing for your first face-to-face contact is centered on the development and clear presentation of this sales pitch.

After an owner agrees to a meeting, your first step is to send, well in advance, introductory material on your company. This should be a customized printed package that is specific to your acquisition process. Many elements are constant for all targets, but there should be some tailoring for each individual prospect. While your package can include sales brochures or an annual report, its main purpose is to express the basic strategy behind your acquisition program: Why are you looking for acquisitions (your "one reason")? Where do you see opportunity? What is the ultimate goal that you have for the acquisition? All of these questions were answered in your strategic planning. Now you need to present them for consumption by the prospect.

You are not, of course, disclosing your proprietary corporate strategy in these documents, but rather giving the prospect's owners a taste of how you see them fitting into the bigger picture of your company's evolution. Your sole purpose at this stage is to arouse their interest. That means you have to summarize your thinking in terms that make sense from the seller's point of view. As you move forward in negotiations, you can peel back the onion to reveal your more detailed plans.

The introductory material you send allows the prospect to become more familiar with your team and operations. For example, if you are a $100 million division of a larger company, you should highlight your division's capabilities and the people running it. You might include an organizational chart so the prospect has a sense of how the division and its management fit within the larger structure of the parent company. Depending on your comfort level and legal disclosure guidelines, you can include as much or as little financial information as you want. The introductory package should have the look of your other corporate materials to maintain consistency with your brand. To that end, I often have my client's corporate marketing department design the piece with direction from the acquisition team.

BE THEIR GUEST

Who should attend this first meeting with a prospect? I generally recommend a combination of the Acquisition Coordinator, perhaps one other member of the A-Team, and your third-party adviser. Bringing the third-party adviser along is beneficial for a couple of reasons. First, the adviser was often the initial point of contact with the prospect, so there is already some history established. Second, the adviser has attended dozens, even hundreds, of these types of meetings, so she knows how to keep the conversation focused.

Once the date and time of the visit is set, contact the owner of the target company and request recommendations on where to stay. Also ask for suggestions of a place to meet for dinner the night before the meeting. There is a reason for this step. You will be amazed at how much you can learn by making the owner feel like he is the host of the visit. Does he go the extra mile to help you make reservations at the best nearby hotel? Does he give detailed directions (or even send a car) to pick you up at the airport? This is particularly telling if the target company is in a small town and the nearest airport is two hours away. By deferring to the owner for the logistical arrangements, you are not only building trust between the two parties but also learning about his mindset. You get a sense of personal values and of how serious the prospect is about the forthcoming discussions.

I accompanied one client on a visit to a prospect located in a small Vermont town, ninety minutes from the closest major airport. The owner sent a driver to pick us up because he knew it would be difficult for us to find his premises along the local back roads. He also set us up at a bed-and-breakfast in town at a discounted rate. From this, we knew we were dealing with an enthusiastic, savvy owner, and we went on to have an extremely productive meeting. I have also experienced the other side of the equation, where owners were unhelpful and didn't care what impression they might make. One owner forgot to make hotel reservations, while another actually forgot about the meeting entirely and had left for a business trip to Mexico by the time we arrived.

PLANNING THE OUTCOME

A key aspect of your preparation is sitting down with your A-Team and figuring out what you want to learn from this first face-to-face meeting. One approach is to identify your "Top Ten" burning questions about the prospect. Through research, you have already developed a profile of the target company, so where are the holes in your knowledge? These gaps become items for your list. Perhaps you need more clarity about the company's financial health, or more about the management structure—facts you were unable to acquire through your initial phone contacts. You are not trying to perform your entire due diligence in this first meeting. Rather, you are looking for clarity in your impressions of the target company and how it realistically aligns with your prospect criteria. Having the Top Ten in writing serves as a reminder when you are sitting in the meeting and an opportune moment comes to ask a new question.

One way to spur dialogue on the topics about which you need more information is through a PowerPoint presentation. A brief overview introduces you and your thinking about a potential relationship. The PowerPoint slides should be slightly formal (with minimal clip art or flashy transitions) and tailored to the prospect so the owner knows you have put some effort into it. At this point, you could still be meeting and dealing with up to a dozen prospects. Each one should be shown its due respect so you create a level playing field for the purposes of comparison.

The PowerPoint's main purpose is not for you to deliver a lecture but to stimulate a lively conversation. It is essential to create a presentation that is quite different from a typical company sales pitch. I had a client who wanted to show eighty slides devoted entirely to what was wonderful about his own company. No owner wants to sit through that! Owners are far more interested in what you have to say about them. Three slides about your own organization are quite enough, and they should come at the end of the presentation.

Your slides should normally follow a prescribed format that allows for an easy dialogue between buyer and prospect. Think in terms of four short sections with titles something like this:

1. Our Understanding of Your Company
2. Why We Are Here
3. Next Steps
4. About Our Company

The first section, "Our Understanding of Your Company," serves to demonstrate that you have taken the trouble to learn about your host's operation. But it has another, more artful purpose. You are enticing the owner to correct and expand on your current information. For this reason, you want to build these slides around your predefined prospect criteria and Top Ten list of questions. For example, if company size is an important criterion, include a slide that estimates the prospect's revenue. If you don't know, guess low. If you guess high, then the owner will often agree with you. If you guess low, though, the owner will generally correct you with a more accurate figure. You can elicit valuable information through this simple technique.

The second section, "Why We Are Here," is effectively your sales pitch. It is your opportunity to sketch out in general terms a vision of growth and success based on a combination of the two entities.

The third section, "Next Steps," is a specific call to action. You need to be clear about what you want the owner to do following the first meeting. Very likely, this is a return visit to your company premises.

The fourth section, "About Our Company," is where you provide an overview of your own enterprise. Here, it's important to focus on aspects that reinforce your strategic vision and make sense of your reason for being there. In other words, think in terms of what might interest the owner you are talking to. Remember that this isn't a prospective customer for your products, but rather a potential collaborator in the process of an acquisition.

Your PowerPoint presentation should be succinct and to the point. Its only function is to help guide a general discussion of the vision you see for the union of the two companies.

In addition to the PowerPoint, you should create a paper handout. This should include a printout of the PowerPoint slides, with possibly some extra pages of detail. Whether or not you leave the handout behind depends on your assessment of the meeting's success. You have the option to leave it or not.

Now, while you should always have a PowerPoint prepared, there are situations when you decide not to deploy it. If you are meeting the owner in a small office with just one or two people present, or if the location isn't suitable for a presentation—for example, a private home—you can use a flipchart instead or simply work from the printed handout, which should also be prepared in advance.

As you plan the encounter, bear in mind that this is only the first of what could be dozens of meetings. Thus, you don't have to accomplish everything at once. In fact, I suggest that the initial visit consist of no more than dinner the night before and a three-hour meeting the next morning. Specifically, avoid having breakfast with the owner, and do not stay for lunch. Limiting the time you spend together on the first visit will help you avoid getting in too deep, too fast. If you spend too long with the owner, you will end up talking about subjects you'd rather not have broached, or you will find yourself having to fill dead space. A short first meeting whets the prospect's appetite without providing enough answers for a premature decision one way or the other.

MEETING THE PROSPECT

The night before the meeting, I recommend that you sit down to dinner with the owner and whomever else he might wish to bring along at a venue of his choosing. The owner's choice of restaurant gives another indication of his personal style, while also making him the host in an environment comfortable to him. Accompanying my clients to these first meetings, I have dined everywhere from fine steakhouses to fast-food restaurants. One owner invited us to a strip club. Needless to say, a CEO who wants to take two people he has just met to a strip club the night before a business meeting sends a strong message about his value system. We didn't schedule a follow-up meeting.

During dinner, allow the conversation to range widely. I often prefer not to focus on business. Take this as an opportunity to show your personal side and humanize yourself. Talk about your children or where you went to college. In order to gain the trust of the seller, you must be seen as more than a person with a checkbook. You can offer to pay for the dinner, but it is fine to graciously accept if the prospect pays. These little moments are all about establishing trust. Remember, you are not going to buy the company over dinner. What you are doing is building rapport.

After dinner, debrief with your colleagues and third-party adviser. Based on new information you have learned from the owner, you can adjust your meeting agenda and your PowerPoint presentation for the next morning.

Have breakfast with your team alone to limit the time you spend with the prospect. As for the meeting itself, it should not run beyond three hours in total. I usually suggest to the owner that we start with a tour of the facility. Beginning with a tour can help guide the questions at the sit-down session that follows, as well as take some of the stuffiness out of the meeting as you walk around with your hosts and meet other members of the organization.

When you finally do sit down and begin your PowerPoint presentation, remember that you are there to have a dialogue. Most likely, you are dealing with someone who says his company is still "not for sale." In his mind, he has agreed to this meeting out of courtesy, but he still believes that he is not actually going to end up selling. That is why the idea of a dialogue is so important. You can say, right at the beginning:

> "I understand you are not for sale—you've made that clear, and we didn't think you were for sale. What we want to do today is spend some time having a dialogue about why we think a union makes sense, explain our interest, and explore some possibilities with you."

A statement like this immediately disarms the seller and takes the pressure out of the meeting. Remember, when someone says her company is not for sale, it is usually just a defense mechanism. By acknowledging and respecting these natural apprehensions, you can put the seller at ease, even though, in your mind, you know that her company actually *is* for sale—for the right equation.

Throughout the meeting, using your PowerPoint as a guide, you want the prospect to describe his business: what the company does, how it operates, who its customers are. You are not only looking to tick off boxes for your prospect criteria. You are also trying to discern the company DNA, the soul of the business. If the owner says, "We are the low-cost guy in the market" or "We put a huge emphasis on training," you are learning about the company's values and brand position. You may have a sense of that from a website or brochure, but now you are able to confirm or adjust your impressions, and you can follow up with questions. You can get a sense of the management team simply by listening to how the owner describes them. Even who gets mentioned first can give you clues. For example, if you say, "Tell us about your people," and the owner launches into describing the fantastic new floor manager whom he just hired away from a competitor, it tells you he is close to his operations and values the skills of lower-level personnel just as much as a CFO or marketing VP.

While you are listening and coaxing information from the prospect about his business, you must be prepared to give up some information about your own company. Generally, it is easier to ask someone questions if you are willing to disclose something about yourself. You will naturally set a limit on how much you are willing to divulge, but you don't want the conversation to feel like a one-way street. This is particularly true in the financial area. The less you ask about the prospect's financials, the more you impress him about your intent: You show him that you are focused on the strategic vision. At the first meeting, I usually discuss only high-level financials such as revenues and maybe one other financial parameter, such as gross margins. This is another reason to keep meetings short. If you are in the conference room too long, you risk drifting into a discussion of price—a major error at this stage in the relationship. As we have established earlier, avoiding "the price trap" is one of the keys to successfully negotiating a company acquisition.

HOSTING THE SECOND MEETING

Wrap up your meeting before lunch, thank your hosts for the visit, and let them know you will be back in touch within a week. Discuss with your third-party adviser your general impressions of the meeting and the feel you got for the prospect. From a dinner plus a three-hour conference and tour, you should have acquired a good sense of what the company is about and how it is run.

Once you are back at your office, you can sit down with your entire A-Team and conduct a full debriefing session. Share what you learned from your time with the prospect and fill in your Prospect Profile with new information. Continuing to use your prospect criteria as your guide, decide with the A-Team if you want to move the prospect down the Prospect Funnel and hold another meeting—this time, a return visit by the owner to your facility.

If you decide to move forward and host the prospect for that second meeting, it should follow a similar format to your visit to the prospect. Pick a place for dinner the night before, and the next morning conduct a short meeting, including a tour of your premises. This return visit provides an opportunity to continue building trust. By having the prospect as your guest and taking him on a tour, you are divulging more information about yourself and your company. You can introduce the prospect to key members of your acquisition team so he becomes more familiar with the leaders in your organization. Your CEO can make a brief "pop-in" appearance, but I suggest you continue holding her back for later in the negotiating process. Remember, one of the CEO's roles is that of "closer," used to bring weight and seriousness to negotiations when needed.

CONTINUING THE COURTSHIP

After the return visit, it is time for another debriefing with the A-Team. With each phone call and meeting, you are learning more and more about the prospect. Using this new information, along with what you have previously gleaned through your research, you and your A-Team are constantly reevaluating. If you decide to proceed with certain prospects, then move them down the Prospect Funnel and into deeper negotiations.

In this chapter, we have given what may seem disproportionate attention to a single meeting. However, such attention is definitely warranted. The experience of my firm has shown repeatedly how critical the early face-to-face encounters between buyer and seller can turn out to be. Company acquisition is a relationship-driven process, and this is where the foundation of trust is laid down—or not, as the case may be. The handling of the logistics, planning, and execution of the first meetings reveals volumes about both parties to each other. That's why this step is so rich in opportunities for the savvy buyer.

Step-by-step, you are drawing closer to a union of companies that will help your business grow. You are also getting into trickier territory, as hard numbers begin to be discussed. In Chapter 9, we explore the best methods to assess a company's value—both financial and otherwise—in order to give you optimum advantage at the negotiating table.

CHAPTER 9

FIRST ASSESSMENTS

AFTER TWO FACE-TO-FACE MEETINGS and numerous phone calls, you are developing a strong personal impression of the target company. Through your on-site visit, the owner's return visit, as well as many other follow-up conversations, you have been building trust and on that basis have elicited a growing body of information. This should be reflected in an increasingly detailed Prospect Profile, as discussed in Chapter 6.

Now is the time for your A-Team to make a formal assessment of the prospect so that you can decide whether or not to embark on serious negotiations. There are two components of the assessment: evaluation and valuation. Though distinct, they are often confused. In this chapter, we begin by delineating the difference between them. Next, we explore evaluation and valuation in depth as they relate to your strategic objectives. Then, we briefly don our accounting hats to review some of the formulas and methodologies that go into a typical valuation.

EVALUATION VS. VALUATION

Evaluation answers two key questions:

1. Is this company a good strategic fit?
2. Does this company match my one reason to buy?

The primary method for conducting evaluations is rating the company against the acquisition criteria that your A-Team drew up (see Chapter 3). Recall from Chapter 5 that each criterion carries a specific metric and a weighted value for scoring. Needless to say, your assessment of a company includes many components that are not necessarily financial, even though you have given them a metric in order to create your scoring system for prospects. These are the components that evaluation addresses.

Valuation refers to the specifically financial component of the equation: It defines the economic value you place on the company. We will see later in this chapter that valuation must be further distinguished from price. The key point here is that a complete assessment of a prospect includes both nonfinancial (evaluation) and financial (valuation) elements.

Together, evaluation and valuation provide the two main planks for your negotiation platform, in the event you do decide to pursue the prospect.

EVALUATION: DATA VS. INTUITION

The formal assessment begins with evaluation, the process of assessing whether the target company can meet your strategic objectives. In reality, you have been conducting evaluations continually since putting together your initial list of companies, prioritizing and reprioritizing them based on your acquisition criteria. Now you are approaching a key choice point. Will you initiate active negotiations for a purchase? Will you start asking questions—including the financial ones—that up until now you have held back?

You want to make the decision to proceed as objective as possible, and that's the purpose of your acquisition criteria. You may recall that I suggested developing your criteria along functional lines, with specific metrics for management, production, marketing, finance, etc. The same principle applies when you are evaluating companies at this critical stage in the acquisition process. Now that you have exchanged visits, you should be able to get a vivid sense of how one target company compares with another in its manufacturing process or sales force or any other area of the business. Focusing your discussions with the A-Team on functional areas facilitates clearer and more objective comparisons between companies.

Your acquisition criteria are designed to bring objectivity to all aspects of the prospect evaluation, including the most intangible issues, such as company culture, and the most uncertain questions, such as future demand. In using the criteria, your aim is to generate a numerical score that can stand as a buttress against impulsive excitement, aversion, or anxiety. Nevertheless, you should never let the numbers alone dictate your decisions.

As my clients collect more and more concrete data in order to gain an objective comparison of prospects, I counsel them to listen to their gut feelings about a prospect. Particularly at the stage when you are seriously considering only a handful of prospects, there may be only small differences in the objective scoring of prospects. When you rate them numerically, your top two or three prospects may be nearly identical in how well they fit your acquisition criteria. As you ask yourself which prospect to move forward with first, you should balance these metric scores with your intuitive impressions of the company. What did you take away from your meetings and phone interactions? What feeling did you get about each prospect? What was your sense of the company DNA, of the owner's attitude, of the general atmosphere? A prospect who is lukewarm to the idea of a union may score slightly higher, based on your listed criteria, than a prospect who is genuinely enthused by the idea. In that case, you may prefer to invest your efforts in the more enthusiastic (but slightly lower-scoring) prospect.

I want to emphasize that "going with your gut" is a maxim to be used with caution. Objectivity is still your strongest asset when evaluating and comparing prospects. Your predefined acquisition criteria are still the best guide to prioritizing prospects. When members of the A-Team disagree about the status of a prospect, your first look should be back to the criteria to see how closely the target really fits each metric. By carefully reviewing the data you've uncovered and the resulting scores, you should be able to reach a consensus on prioritization. Intuition should be introduced only as a tiebreaker when there are very small differences in the objective scoring of prospects or an unresolved conflict of views. If team disagreements persist, you can invite the CEO to step in and receive a summary of the dispute in order to issue a final ruling.

VALUATION: AN ART, NOT A SCIENCE

We now turn to valuation—establishing the financial worth of the company. This does not mean you should abandon the ongoing process of evaluation. As you begin to review the financial picture, you must be careful to continue your efforts to assess the prospect for its strategic fit. Too often, I have seen clients launch into the financial aspects of a deal and lose their focus on the strategic underpinnings of the union. They become hypnotized by numbers and begin obsessively hunting for a "deal." They spend weeks poring over Microsoft Excel spreadsheets to arrive at precisely the wrong answer. I always have to remind them that, in the long run, it is more expensive to buy the wrong company cheap than to overpay for the right one.

Valuation is an art, not a science. As we shall see, there are many ways to calculate a company's financial value, and none of them is perfect. No software or algorithm delivers a single, indisputable number. Depending on which valuation method is used, a company's value can fluctuate by millions of dollars. This is why the valuation process requires special patience and the willingness to adopt multiple perspectives. To complicate matters further, when valuing a company for the purposes of acquisition, your calculations are largely predicated on future performance, which is by definition uncertain.

Despite these difficulties, valuation is a critical tool in business. It is not only necessary for acquisitions but also for a variety of other transactions such as divestitures, as well as for defense against hostile takeovers, debt offerings, and many other situations. Because it is such a vital and yet complex process, there are lengthy textbooks and MBA courses on valuation. For this reason, you may need the expert help of an outside consultant as you enter this phase. My purpose here is not to explain all the sophisticated methods of business valuation but rather to help you understand the critical role valuation plays in the acquisition process.

VALUE VS. PRICE

In the context of acquisitions, any discussion of valuation has to begin with the understanding that *valuation* and *price* have different meanings and are (usually) two quite different numbers. A company's *valuation* is the financial assessment of a business determined by one or more accepted methods of calculation. Its main purpose is to establish an indication of what you should pay for the prospect. The *price* is the dollar amount that will be negotiated in the acquisition agreement.

Remember the core premise of our Roadmap approach to acquisition: Every company is for sale for the right equation. The valuation certainly forms a major part of that equation, but there is no reason to assume it will be all of it. One of the factors that often must be mitigated is the owner's ego. For example, your valuation methods may place the value of a company at $35 million, but the owner may passionately believe her company is worth at least $40 million. When constructing your initial offer, you may have reason to take into account the owner's expectation of what she will get for her company (see Figure 9-1). Other factors that can force a gap between price and value include historic transaction multiples in the industry, revenue replacement issues, and even the rumor mill.

CONVENTIONAL VALUATION

I want to emphasize that valuation should be anchored in your strategic rationale for buying another company in the first place. It all comes back to your business strategy and the synergies that will be created by the union of two companies. Valuation is an exercise in predicting the future, and the underlying question your process addresses should be: What will those synergies be worth in two, five, or even ten years?

Take, for example, a client of mine who was interested in buying a company with federal government contracts with the Department of Homeland Security (DHS). His main strategic rationale for the acquisition was to gain a foothold in Homeland Security contracting. Therefore, a prospect's value to my client was largely dependent on how well it was currently entrenched with DHS, but more

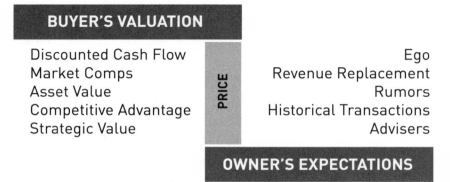

Figure 9-1. The buyer's valuation vs. the owner's expectations.

importantly, how well it would be in the future. A prospect with 10 percent of its business with DHS could prove more valuable to my client than a prospect with 80 percent of its business with DHS. This would be the case if the 80 percent prospect's contracts were expiring or low-revenue and the 10 percent prospect had a long-term contract with steady, high revenues and the likelihood of more contracts to come. You can see from this example how the calculation of each prospect's value must be adjusted based upon the predicted synergies that it would bring to the union, not just its current financial performance.

Needless to say, with so much hanging on future outcomes, the quality and quantity of your research become paramount. The more information you are armed with, the clearer the picture in your crystal ball.

There is a further complication you must anticipate: the probability that you are using incomplete financial information from the prospect, at least at first. While you are still building the relationship and before you have signed a Letter of Intent, it is unlikely the prospect will hand over the complete books on the company. Nevertheless, you can put together a reasonably accurate picture of the company's value absent the detailed financials. This is where your listening and investigative skills come into play. You can construct a provisional valuation from various fragments of suggestive data. These might include the number of employees, size of the facility, output quantity, units sold, and rework percentage. Combine those factors with whatever basic financials you have acquired, add your educated guesses about future synergies, and you should be able to make an initial estimate of the prospect's value. (See Figure 9-2.)

THE BUYER'S EQUATION

Throughout our exposition of the Roadmap method, we have given special emphasis to the seller's equation—the total assembly of factors that motivate an owner to sell her company. Conversely, we

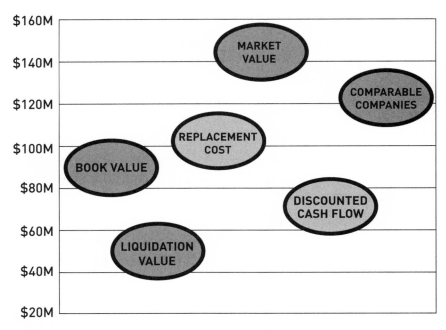

Figure 9-2. Different valuation methods may produce different results.

need to give consideration to what we could call "the buyer's equation." Here is the principle that concerns us: In any transaction, value is determined not just by the product that is being sold but just as much by the person who is making the purchase.

Take an old van with 100,000 miles on its odometer and a few battle scars in its bodywork. In the normal course of things, you might give it a value of, say, $3,000. But suppose you are the owner of an ambitious pastry company that has just landed a contract to serve a chain of hotels throughout New York. Your contract is worth $500,000, but it depends on perfect performance starting tomorrow. You need a reliable vehicle to make deliveries. How much might you pay for that battered old van right now? $5,000? $10,000? $20,000? By the same token, in the M&A market, the buyer's situation impacts the value of an acquisition as much as the apparent worth of the target company. It's important to hold this in mind as we dive into the intricacies of valuation.

THE MULTIDIMENSIONAL APPROACH TO VALUATION

You will discover that there is no one right method for determining a company's financial value. Depending on the method you use, you will almost certainly get different results. Not only are there many methods; there are several variants of each technique, all with their own algorithms and complexities. Let's list just some of the most common methods used:

- Discounted cash flow
- Liquidation value
- Completed transaction comparables
- Book value
- Guideline public company multiples

With so many possible approaches, the task of valuation can seem daunting, especially because the whole operation depends on your predictions of future conditions and the vagaries of incomplete data. Given the challenges, I recommend a balanced approach drawing on the first three methods in our menu of possible techniques given above. These three techniques, which we explore below, work well together because the first is based on the prospect's income statement, the second on its balance sheet, and the third on a review of what is happening in the prospect's market. You will most likely arrive at a different value for each of the three selected methods. You can then triangulate, reconcile, and weight these results to arrive at a single number for your valuation.

Method 1: Discounted Cash Flow

The first valuation method—discounted cash flow (DCF)—is one of the most popular because it takes account of the future prospects, not just the historical performance of the company. DCF bases the valuation of a business on the net *present* value of *projected* cash flows. Future cash flows are given a present-day value by applying a discount rate specific to your target company.

To understand DCF, let's first establish some basic concepts. As everyone knows, a dollar you hold today is worth more than a dollar you expect to have five years from now. That's why, in the consumer world, one always pays more for an installment plan than for an immediate cash purchase. When you are buying a company, you are buying future benefit, so it is important to have a way to measure the impact of time on value. This is the purpose of DCF. It's a precise way of measuring the reduced worth of future money, by applying a discount percentage. This opens the question of what the discount should be.

To determine the discount rate, we use a tool called WACC: the Weighted Average Cost of Capital. Here's why. When capital costs are high, your risks increase, and you therefore need to reduce your valuation of future cash flows. This in turn will reduce the amount you are willing to pay for a company. If capital costs are low, you can afford to increase the future valuation of cash flows, and you therefore may be willing to pay more for an acquisition.

But whose cost of capital are you looking at? In the first place, it's your own WACC, as the buyer, that needs to be examined, because this provides a measure of the demands placed on your financial structure by a new acquisition. You also want to run a calculation of WACC for the target company, so you get a closer understanding of the level of risk in the purchase. Finally, if you find yourself in a bidding war with other buyers, you may want to estimate their WACC, because this gives you an indication of their relative strength. If you run into a competitor whose cost of capital is far lower than your own, you may just decide to back out of the deal, because they can afford to pay significantly more.

Debt and Equity

WACC gives you a way to look at the capital structure of a company. It considers two familiar kinds of capital: debt and equity. Each has its own costs. The cost of debt is easy to identify. It's the interest you pay on a loan. The cost of equity is a little trickier. Here you are concerned with the question: *What would I have to give up to entice investors to put their money into this company, as compared with other investment vehicles they might choose?*

The classic way to assess the cost of equity is to use a tool called Beta. This measures the volatility of a company's value, compared to the overall market in companies. On the stock market, Beta measures the difference between the volatility of a particular share and the volatility of the stock market as a whole. A high Beta indicates that the share prices swing up and down more than the stock market index. A low Beta suggests the share in question closely tracks the market as a whole. The large blue chips tend to reflect the overall index and therefore have a low Beta. In contrast, an exciting new technology company, showing great share price volatility, may have a very high Beta. (It's worth noting that smaller companies tend to have a higher Beta simply by virtue of their size.) In terms of valuation, high Beta indicates high risk; therefore, as Beta increases, so does the cost of equity. That will be factored into the WACC equation, which in turn will determine the DCF and ultimately the valuation.

When dealing with a privately held company, you have to make your best estimate of its Beta by drawing on public information. One way is to select a "proxy" for the company among equivalent publicly traded entities. If that proves impossible, you can adopt the average Beta for the entire industry.

WACC weights both the cost of equity and the cost of debt

based on the capital structure of the company. It weights them depending on the balance of the equity and debt in the capitalization of the particular company. In theory, the resulting formula tells you how much interest you would have to pay for every dollar you finance. This will drive your estimate of DCF (the value of future cash flows), and that in turn will give you a specific number for your valuation of the company.

Recall that we recommend using several methods of valuation, not just one. Calculating valuation based on DCF and WACC gives you just one perspective, not a final answer. Nevertheless, a special benefit of using WACC is that it indicates the maximum that you should be willing to pay for a company—your price ceiling—based on the assumptions of future performance included in the DCF.

Doing the Math

The correct use of WACC requires some degree of finance skill and needs the help of experts, whether in-house or from outside. If math makes your head spin, you may want to skip this brief section on how to calculate WACC. However, even if you are not an expert in finance or accounting, I still encourage anyone considering an acquisition to gain a basic understanding of how WACC is determined.

Let's start with the formula. The important point here is to understand that WACC is not just the after-tax cost of debt. WACC is the weighted cost of all sources of capital for a company—both debt and equity. (See Figure 9-3.)

WEIGHTED AVERAGE COST OF CAPITAL

> COST OF EQUITY + COST OF DEBT

Figure 9-3. WACC.

Clearly, the picture is going to be impacted by the relative pro-portions of debt and equity that make up the company's capital, so we build that into the equation:

$$\textbf{WACC} = \textbf{(Cost of Equity) (\%Equity)} + \textbf{(Cost of Debt) (\%Debt)}$$

Now let's delve a little deeper. The cost of *equity* (K_e) has the following formula:

$$\textbf{K}_e = \textbf{R}_f + \boldsymbol{\beta}(\textbf{R}_m - \textbf{R}_f) * \textbf{(\%Capitalization that is equity)}$$

Here is what the terms mean:

- **R_f** = The risk-free rate of return (this is usually determined by the current rate on a 20-year treasury bill)
- **R_m** = Market return (this is the historic average rate of return on the stock market)
- **β** = Beta (as we have indicated, this is a risk factor, measuring volatility of a company in relation to the market)

The cost of debt has the following formula:

$$\textbf{K}_d = [i * (\textbf{1} - \textbf{Tax rate})] * \textbf{(\%Capitalization that is debt)}$$

The terms here are:

- **K_d** = Cost of debt
- **i** = Long-term interest/Long-term debt
- **Tax rate** = The effective tax rate of the company

You can see, then, that WACC is dependent upon a number of factors, some of which are market-specific (the risk-free rate and market return) and some of which are company-specific (Beta, tax rate, and long-term interest and debt). These variables can cause a great deal of turmoil, as even the "constants" of the market specifics can be manipulated. It is important that as you go through the formula, you keep precise records of how and why you came to a particular number for any of the variables.

Adjusting for Risk

The story of WACC isn't complete until you've taken account of the level of risk involved in your acquisition. The lowest risk is usually associated with buying a direct competitor. Here, you are dealing with familiar products in a familiar market. A higher risk is associated with an acquisition that entails new products or that takes you into unfamiliar markets. And the highest risk of all is an acquisition that takes you outside your company experience in both products and markets.

The risk factor needs to be given a numerical value, and once established, that number is used to adjust your calculation of the cost of capital, or WACC. The adjustment is actually a matter of common sense. The greater your risk, the less you should be willing to pay for an acquisition. A more precise analysis of risk can be achieved using what is known as the "build up" method, which measures risk in relation to size of company, industry, anticipated future performance, etc.

With all these equations, it's worth remembering that a general measure of WACC is what concerns you, not the minute discrepancies that may result from complex calculations. As I've indicated, there are many excellent sources on the intricacies of company valuation. My purpose in this book is to establish the fundamental principles that should guide your decisions.

Discounted cash flow is far from a perfect method. Again, you are predicting outcomes, and there is inherent uncertainty in such projections. Nevertheless, DCF has two significant benefits: It accounts for the future, and it addresses cash flows. In addition, DCF keys in on the operational efficiency of a business and recognizes the time value of money. That's why I, along with most valuation professionals, recommend discounted cash flow as an essential part of any valuation process.

Method 2: Liquidation Value

The second method I recommend is liquidation value (see Figure 9-4). The question this approach answers is: What would the company be worth if it closed down today? Here you estimate the value of the assets the prospect holds, particularly if the company owns real estate or large pieces of capital equipment. Capital equipment may have depreciated but can still add value to the balance sheet. Precisely identifying the total assets of the prospect can be difficult in the early stages, but you can make educated guesses if you conduct thorough research and listen carefully to what the owner says.

What you are essentially trying to do with this approach is understand the difference between the current market value of the target's assets and the company's "book value"—that is, the value the assets have been given in the company's accounts. This can be useful for companies that are not making a profit, for companies

> ✔ Cash Assets @ 100%
>
> ✔ Accounts Receivable @ 85%
>
> ✔ Inventory: Raw Materials/Finished Goods @ 50%-60%
>
> ✔ Machinery & Equipment @ 50%-60% of Appraisal
>
> ✔ Real Estate @ 40%-70% of Appraisal
>
> ✔ Less All Liabilities @ 100%

Figure 9-4. An example of liquidation value.

with unused assets such as real estate or machinery, and for businesses that will be shut down. Calculating the liquidation value gives you a better idea of what a bank might lend in the form of an asset-based loan. This in turn will indicate a "floor" value—the least the company is realistically worth.

Method 3: Completed Transaction Comparables

The final method we examine here is completed transaction comparables, which are recent deals similar to the one you are contemplating. You can access information on these through a research company such as Mergerstat, Pratt's Stats, or (for small transactions) BIZCOMPS. If you are a food processing company looking to buy a meat supplier, you can search for like deals in your industry and come up with a list of transactions that give a purchase price along with basic financials for the buyer and the seller. You will then have enough information to determine a value for your prospect by comparing what you know of the company with the already completed deals in which other meat suppliers were bought. Of course, you have to make adjustments for any number of factors, as no previous deal is going to be exactly the same as yours. Still, transaction comps often serve as a healthy "reality check" when starting to assess the financial picture. They can give you a perspective on what is happening in the same market space in which your deal would take place. They have another very useful function, too. You can be sure that the owner of your target company has researched similar transactions, so the comps give you a valuable clue as to the price the seller is expecting to receive.

I must reiterate that no single valuation method will give you the definitive value of a business (look back at Figure 9-2). As mentioned earlier in the chapter but bears repeating, valuation is an art, not a science. This is why you paint your financial picture of the prospect using multiple valuation methods. You then combine this picture with the many other factors—tangible and intangible—that make up the all-important equation for which the owner will sell. Once you have established a valuation, using every appropriate tool at your disposal, you are ready to calculate an initial offering price. (See Figure 9-5 for a summary of valuation methods.)

RULES OF THUMB

Thinking about valuation is bound to be affected by the traditional "rules of thumb" that are frequently repeated in conversations about M&A. For instance, you often hear the statement "We'll pay between five and seven times for a company." This calls for explanation. Five to seven times what?

Normally, what's referred to here is EBITDA: earnings before interest, taxes, depreciation, and amortization. EBITDA provides the closest proximity to actual cash flow. Paying five times EBITDA

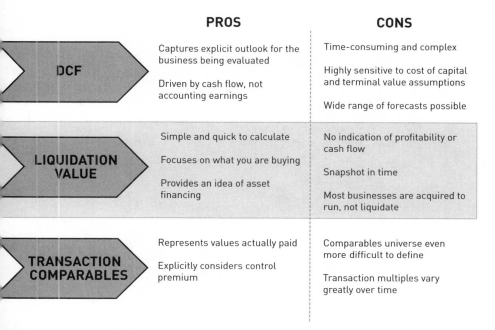

	PROS	CONS
DCF	Captures explicit outlook for the business being evaluated Driven by cash flow, not accounting earnings	Time-consuming and complex Highly sensitive to cost of capital and terminal value assumptions Wide range of forecasts possible
LIQUIDATION VALUE	Simple and quick to calculate Focuses on what you are buying Provides an idea of asset financing	No indication of profitability or cash flow Snapshot in time Most businesses are acquired to run, not liquidate
TRANSACTION COMPARABLES	Represents values actually paid Explicitly considers control premium	Comparables universe even more difficult to define Transaction multiples vary greatly over time

Figure 9-5. A summary of valuation methods.

is another way of saying that you expect a 20 percent return on your money. That's to say, you expect to get $1 for every $5 that you invest, with all your money returned within five years. So when buyers speak of paying five to seven times EBITDA, they are indicating a target return of 15 to 20 percent.

Here is where we need to recall "the buyer's equation." Past EBITDA is of course a fixed quantity. But future EBITDA is a pure projection, and it can vary wildly according to who is making the calculation. One buyer may have the capacity to massively increase the earnings of an acquisition, while another is content just to sustain the current rate of EBITDA.

This difference is rarely mentioned in discussions of M&A, yet it can be one of the most decisive factors in a valuation. When it comes to acquiring companies, who is doing the buying can be every bit as important as what is being bought.

ON TO DEEPER NEGOTIATION

We've established here the critical distinctions between evaluation and valuation, and between valuation and price. We've also recommended a combination of three valuation methods: discounted cash flow, liquidation value, and completed transaction comparables.

The next chapter is explicitly devoted to negotiating tactics and moving the process forward with your top prospects. You have worked hard to build a relationship based on trust and the vision of a bright new future for two companies. Now, you are preparing to construct a solid deal that will ensure your hard work produces the optimal result: a union of two companies stronger together than they were apart.

CHAPTER 10

NEGOTIATING
WITH PROSPECTS

NOW THAT YOU HAVE COMPLETED in-depth evaluations (your strategic assessment), coupled with initial valuations (the financial dimension), you are ready to begin negotiating with the most promising prospects. Your primary goal for negotiations is to have the decision makers in each organization—yours and the prospect's—come into alignment with the overarching strategy behind the deal. Once both sides are excited about the possibilities of the union, the minutiae can be hammered out. If you always keep the master plan in perspective, the wrangling over the details will be considerably less acrimonious and more productive.

When approaching negotiation for an acquisition, it's essential to establish the right mindset from the start. As we unfold the process here, we'll be constantly attentive to the balance you must strike between negotiating firmly on the one hand and protecting your relationship with the prospect on the other. In this chapter, we begin by building what we call your "Negotiation Platform." Next, we look at how to be effective when sitting across the table from your prospect. We conclude by discussing the role of outside advisers as you negotiate, including how to effectively use your advisers while helping the prospect find his own expert support in the process.

Remember that negotiating an acquisition is all about finding the right equation for the owner to sell. Your prior interactions with the prospect, both in person and on the phone, continue to serve you well here. Understanding the DNA of the target company and the owner's personal priorities will help you find that all-important equation.

BUILDING YOUR NEGOTIATION PLATFORM

Before you sit across the table from a business owner, you should first sit around the table with your A-Team. Your objective is to develop your Negotiation Platform (see Figure 10-1). This written document is an essential tool to keep you focused on your strategic outcomes while you engage in the push and pull of negotiating a

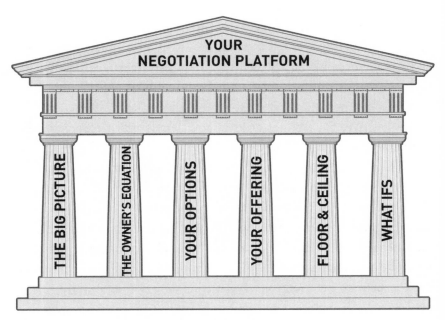

Figure 10-1. Building your Negotiation Platform.

deal. It summarizes your objectives and the basic tactics you will employ throughout the coming process.

The Negotiation Platform is derived from your answers to six key questions:

1. **What is the "big picture"?** The answer to this question can be found way back at the beginning of the acquisition process—your one reason to buy. As you enter negotiations, you want to structure the deal to make sure it fits your single chosen objective. For example, if you are acquiring a company in order to add management depth and experience, you want to ensure that retention of the management team is part of the deal.

2. **What elements of the owner's equation do you already know?** By this point, you should know many of the variables in the equation that would prompt the owner to sell, based on your extensive research coupled with multiple conversations with the prospect. Much of your Negotiation Platform should be designed to lock down these variables, so it makes sense to explore them in depth with your A-Team.

3. **What are your options?** You need to know what happens if the deal falls through or the cost of the seller's equation is just too high. You may recalibrate the deal to acquire a minority interest or look to sign an exclusive manufacturing arrangement with the prospect. You need to keep alternatives in mind, including the possibility of moving on to acquire another company in your Prospect Funnel.

4. **What do you have to offer (in addition to cash)?** Here you review all the known "tradables"—that is, potential components of the acquisition equation. In addition to cash, tradables could include such things as car payments for the owner or keeping family members employed. You need to list and prioritize these in order, summarizing what you are most willing to give up down to what you are least willing to accommodate. As the tradables surface in negoti-

ations, you will be prepared to quickly decide what to give up and what to insist on.

5. What is their floor and what is your ceiling? What is the lowest number the seller will accept, and at what point will you walk away from the deal? This doesn't mean you won't come back to reconsider, but setting a limit beforehand (and sticking to it) allows you to take much of the emotion out of a decision to terminate the negotiations.

6. What if . . . ? With your A-Team, try to imagine some unusual scenarios that may arise and how you would respond. I've had owners come to the table with atypical proposals, such as keeping their entire staff for twelve months or guaranteeing first-class travel for the remainder of their time with the company. While you might not think of these specific situations, anticipating an owner's unusual requests based on your impressions from previous meetings can take some of the shock out of the moment.

Answering these six questions will keep you focused on your desired outcome. The process will be more objective, because you will have already reasoned out your limits and tradables and prepared for scenarios out of left field. You should also have a backup plan in case the deal falls through. Having your answers tabulated in a written Negotiation Platform agreed on by the entire A-Team will give you the advantage of confidence and clarity as you meet with your counterparts at the negotiating table.

BE TOUGH AND PROTECT THE RELATIONSHIP

When my clients transition from the "getting-to-know-you" stage into deeper negotiations with their top prospects, I often have to remind them they are not going off to war. It's understandable that they sometimes think that way, considering the vocabulary that is often employed. After all, we talk about negotiation *tactics*, taking up *positions*, and *fighting* to get what we want in a deal. In reality, any potential deal suffers tremendously when the parties become combative. You can be a tough negotiator and hold the line while protecting your relationship with the prospect. This is particularly important if you are going to continue to work with the seller after the deal is closed. Civility, good humor, and the willingness to listen to the other party's concerns go a long way to protecting the relationship that you have spent months cultivating.

This does not mean you should acquiesce to everything the prospect wants. You haven't come all this way simply to invite her to fill out a blank acquisition agreement. The key to success is knowing when and when not to fight. You will probably have items that are nonnegotiable. You want to save your battles for these items.

A policy of openness and honesty always nurtures the relationship between buyer and seller. If there is disagreement over any point, ask the prospect to help you understand where she is coming from. You may believe that storming off is the best way to "send a message" when a seller won't budge and discussions get heated, but this only produces an atmosphere of mistrust and secrecy. For the best chances of success, you need to create and sustain a positive negotiating environment—and candor is one of the keys to achieving that.

MAKING THE SELLER COMFORTABLE

Just as you did for your first encounter with the seller, you should let him choose the location for meetings, whether it's his executive conference room or an off-site venue in his hometown to maintain some secrecy. Allowing sellers to negotiate on their turf is particularly helpful if you are dealing with a not-for-sale company. As the buyer, you are continually coaxing the seller along, convincing him of the benefits of the transaction. If he is in a familiar setting while this is happening, it only benefits your cause.

You can also make the seller more comfortable by holding back the lawyers. Your initial focus in negotiations should be on how the new combined business will function—not on the legal technicalities of the acquisition agreement. If this is the seller's first time in such a situation (which it usually is), he may feel more comfortable having his lawyer at his side as negotiations begin. In that case, by all means let the seller's lawyer attend. I sometimes joke with my clients that we hope the seller's lawyer can spell *M&A*—because you may well face an attorney with zero experience in the acquisition world. Even so, whatever puts the seller at ease helps the process. Holding your own lawyers in check until you are more deeply in the process can defuse early tensions in the process. If the conversation starts to drift toward legal minutiae before the fundamentals of the business framework are worked out, try to steer the conversation out of the legal jungle and back to the business issues.

TERMS, TIMING, AND TALENT

Once you have developed your Negotiation Platform and created a comfortable environment for the seller, you can begin to stake out the details of the acquisition. I recommend that this be done in three major areas: terms, timing, and talent. The *terms* include the type of deal that will take place and the purchase price. *Timing* refers to the agreed dates for milestones remaining in the acquisition process, such as due diligence and closing. *Talent* not only entails what happens to the employees in each organization but also other resources such as the facilities and capital equipment. With each of these areas, your predefined acquisition criteria should shape your negotiating objectives. For example, if your criteria included a company with an experienced sales force (in the *talent* spectrum), then you should ensure that the prospect's sales force stays intact after the deal is complete.

As you use these three categories to hammer out the detailed structure of the new business, address any of the seller's issues as early as possible. This is another way in which all of your previous research about the owner and her hot buttons will prove inestimably valuable. If you know the seller is worried about how the new management team will be structured, address it directly and talk it through until you reach a firm consensus decision. If you merely say, "We'll take care of that later" and push issues to the side, you show a lack of respect for the seller's concerns. More important, you are storing up trouble for the final and most testing stages of the process.

SMART BARGAINING

Putting together the right equation to persuade the owner to sell normally requires extensive bargaining. I always tell my clients never to bargain "in series" but rather to negotiate "in parallel." In other words, gather all the points of contention and settle them together. Many negotiators want to successively argue each minute point— first a car lease for the owner's son, then dental insurance for the owner's family, then donations to local civic causes, and so forth. They end up trying to bleed the other side to death by fighting on each and every item regardless of its importance. It has been my experience that negotiations most often succeed when issues are put directly on the table all at once.

I cannot overemphasize the importance of writing everything down during negotiations. We use large easels in a corner of the room. Writing things down can be a useful role for the third-party adviser. Once an item has been discussed and decided upon, have someone from each party initial it to show completion. Maintaining the written record helps to keep everyone on the same page. Without such a record, you run the danger of having two differing versions of what was said and/or agreed upon. If you write down the terms as they are settled, you can avoid a potential dustup later should one of the parties misremember what was actually approved.

For my firm, this discipline has saved more than one deal from disaster. I recall negotiations on behalf of a client for a strategic partnership with a leasing operator. After the first round of talks, we thought we had a deal, only to learn that the "decision makers" we had been bargaining with had no power to make decisions! After some harsh words were exchanged, we finally sat down with the CEO and CFO of the target company. We knew there were some key items that were really important to us, including price, length of the partnership, and capital expenditure. Across the table, they were most concerned about price and operational flexibility. After several days of discussion, we had all the salient points—there were seven at the time—written up on our flipchart. We discussed them together in a single meeting and reached an agreement for each one.

At this point, there was another setback. Before the lawyers could draft the final agreement, our counterparts went through an ownership change. This put the deal on hold for nearly a year. The CEO and CFO from the target company stayed on and eventually reopened negotiations, but they acted as though we were all starting from scratch. Instead of rehashing the negotiations, we gathered everyone into the same room, pulled out our flipchart from more than a year before, and in three hours settled the deal.

Earlier in this chapter, I advised prioritizing your tradables. It's easier to negotiate them when everything is laid out from the start. In this way, when the time comes to bargain over the structure of a particular item, you can trade concessions. For example, you can say, "We're happy to support the civic donations, but not the car lease." This is far more effective and time-efficient than negotiating dozens of such items individually.

BROACHING THE PRICE ISSUE

You may have noticed that I haven't touched on the issue of price yet. As you know, this is one of the fundamental principles of the Roadmap process: The price paid for the target company is only one part of the equation that will get the owner to sell. The rest of the equation involves the structure of the new business and the accom-

NEGOTIATING WITH PROSPECTS   171

panying details. If you are unable to bring together an organizational structure that addresses your acquisition strategy and meets the owner's needs, then any discussion of price is moot.

Still, a discussion of price is inevitable. It does not need to be painful, however, particularly if you have already worked through the key strategic points first. I find that sellers are often disarmed when we insist on getting the strategy right before we enter into discussions of price. It is often the owners who raise the issue first, sometimes apprehensively asking, "So . . . when are we going to talk dollars?" When that happens, a dispassionate discussion is called for, with a presentation and explanation of the valuation numbers you have determined. Your initial goal is for the sellers to understand the thinking behind your valuation of their company and how you have arrived at your initial offer. (We look further at how price is presented in the next chapter.)

AVOIDING CIRCLES

I dread when negotiations start to go in circles. When this happens, I immediately advise my clients to take the lead and help maintain urgency in the process. When negotiations stall over minor points, the two sides can lose focus on the big picture and dig in until they get their way. As the buyer, you want to constantly remind the entire negotiating team of the reasons this deal is going to happen and how it will benefit both companies.

If negotiations stall, one way to maintain big-picture thinking is to use the sales strategy of the "assumptive close": Subtly turn the discussion to business activities after the merger, as if it were a foregone conclusion. For example, if you are buying a company in order to obtain a foothold in a new market, you can revolve discussion around how best to attack that market once the deal is done. Present an idea and ask if the seller sees the situation in the same way.

This point goes back to the idea of "selling the vision." You want the owner to be inspired and excited by the prospect of this new, more powerful entity. When you hit a stall in negotiations, making a call to action in the name of the strategic vision can get discussions back on track.

YOUR ADVISER'S ROLE

Assuming your third-party adviser has been with you throughout the entire acquisition process, there is no reason for that to change once you enter deeper negotiations. The adviser's experience in the acquisition process will help you develop your negotiation strategy, organize the meetings, and maintain a big-picture perspective. At the same time, I caution you not to abdicate to your adviser in negotiations. You are the lead negotiator—not the third-party adviser. As the buyer, you must remain personally invested in the process; otherwise, it can become too easy for you to walk away if negotiations stall.

By now, the seller should be increasingly comfortable with your adviser, given the extent of interaction they have had up to this point. Incidentally, one way to demonstrate good faith in the negotiation process is to help the seller to recruit competent advisers of her own. Making a recommendation for a good M&A lawyer or due diligence expert demonstrates that you are not trying to take advantage of an inexperienced seller. Although it may seem counterintuitive to have strong third-party support for the seller, it actually benefits you in the long run. You will do better dealing with highly qualified advisers who can keep both sides focused on the big picture than you would with inept participants.

PREPARING FOR THE ENDGAME

On the Roadmap, creating your Negotiation Platform marks the transition point from the second phase, *Build the Relationships*, to the third and final phase, *Build the Deal*. Completing the last phase requires the help of legal, valuation, and due diligence experts to resolve the technicalities of bringing two companies together. The work you have done in building the relationship with the prospect will pay off as you navigate the complexities of an acquisition agreement and bring the deal to its conclusion.

Your first step in setting up the transaction is to compose a Letter of Intent. On its face, this seems like a dull legal document, but it is in fact a significant symbolic milestone. This is where we turn next.

PART 3

BUILD THE DEAL

CHAPTER 11

The LOI:
A Gentleman's
Agreement

AS YOU ENTER THE *Build the Deal* phase of the acquisition process, you may be tempted to step back and let the lawyers and accountants take over. By now, you can see the finish line and you might imagine there are only technical details left to work out, best handled by the "experts." I caution against this type of thinking. Throughout this phase, there are numerous opportunities to solidify the relationship you have built with the seller and enrich the synergies that will result from the newly formed business. The Letter of Intent (LOI) is the first of these opportunities. While it serves an important legal purpose, it also brings a new level of commitment and resolve to the deal.

In this chapter, we explore both the overall importance of the LOI as well as its individual elements. We first examine its role in the acquisition process as a major landmark in the relationship between buyer and seller. Next, we put together a Pre-LOI Presentation, which helps hammer out some of the specifics that go into the LOI itself. The remainder of the chapter is devoted to building the Letter of Intent piece by piece, concluding with a detailed list of what you should always, sometimes, and never include.

A KEY MILESTONE

As your negotiations evolve, the Letter of Intent is the next major demarcation in the acquisition process. Its main purpose is to clarify the fundamental terms of the deal before either party commits additional resources (both time and money) to the process. As a legal document, the LOI does not commit either party to finalize the transaction. Its function is to summarize what agreements have been reached regarding the basic structure of the new business, while outlining what remains to be worked through.

In addition to its legal function, the LOI also serves a symbolic purpose. It provides a jump-start (or jump-restart) for the final phase of the acquisition process. With closing now in sight, it is a reminder to both sides of the strategic value of the deal. This means it is a tremendously powerful marketing tool for the deal. It can spur on participants, on either side of the deal, who may have become worn out by difficult negotiations. The LOI also implies a moral obligation for both the buyer and the seller to act in good faith and see the deal through to its conclusion.

In its function as a marketing tool, the LOI has a wide-ranging audience. Apart from the owner (or owners), you are addressing his board of directors, advisers, lawyers, accountants, and other top management. One of the most important readers of the document may be the owner's spouse, who often has a major influence over the momentous decision to sell. While it is necessary for the style and tone of the LOI to remain formal and in some parts to employ legalese, with such a diverse audience, there are portions of the document where more descriptive and unceremonious prose should be used, particularly at the beginning.

There is no magical moment in the acquisition process where you *must* send an LOI. Like a marriage proposal, timing reflects the judgment that you are comfortable with the overall direction and seriously want to move forward with the acquisition. Of course, this is more than just a "gut" feeling—it is based on the quality and outcomes of negotiations so far and your A-Team's assessment of how well the prospect fits your strategic criteria.

THE PRE-LOI PRESENTATION

Before my clients present a draft Letter of Intent to a prospect, I suggest they create what I call a "Pre-LOI Presentation" to ensure that both sides are on the same page. After intense negotiations on the framework of the business, and even with everything written down, there are sometimes miscommunications or misunderstandings on issues. This presentation can smooth out the wrinkles. It usually takes the form of a PowerPoint, though a flipchart can also be used. Typically, there is no leave-behind version. The Pre-LOI Presentation specifies everything on which agreement has been reached, as well as those points on which the two sides haven't yet come to an accord. It thereby creates an opportunity for the seller, in a non-threatening way, to bring up any issues she feels haven't been sufficiently addressed.

The Pre-LOI Presentation generally comprises the following sections:

- **How We Got Here.** This includes information about the strategy behind the deal and a timeline of what has taken place so far (meetings, phone calls, etc.).
- **What We Understand About Your Business.** Here, you provide a detailed look at each functional area of the seller's business.
- **What We Heard Was Important to You.** This is a list of the most important points stressed by the seller, gathered from previous meetings and phone calls.
- **How We're Addressing Your Concerns.** For each of the points in the previous section, you summarize the solution agreed to in negotiations.

- **What Else We've Agreed to So Far.** Here, you note other parts of the new business framework that have been agreed upon, listed by functional area.

- **How We'd Like to Move Forward.** You conclude with a proposed timetable for the final steps: LOI signature, due diligence, integration planning, and deal closure.

When you present the Pre-LOI PowerPoint, it's important to pause as you arrive at each element to give the seller a chance to say "yes" or "no" to what you've written down. If she says "no," take the time to understand her concerns and try to work through a solution. This approach allows you to make course corrections so the deal can stay on track to be completed as efficiently as possible. Your focus, again, is the fundamental structure of the new business—not the price. Price will probably come up during this discussion, and as I indicated in Chapter 10, you should carefully explain the reasoning behind your numbers, backed up with supporting documentation.

The Pre-LOI Presentation also serves as an opportunity to elicit more clarity and precision from the seller. Your summary and comments may provoke useful corrections from the owner that reveal more about her company and situation. Throughout the negotiation process, you are still striving to collect any and every bit of relevant data on the prospect. Just because you are moving deeper into negotiations does not mean your process of data collection and evaluation stops. Many prospects are unwilling to divulge more detailed operational or financial information until after the LOI is signed. Even so, this should not prevent you from digging for nuggets during every interaction with the prospect.

After you have completed the Pre-LOI Presentation, all of the interested parties should be on the same page moving forward. At this point, you can begin to draft the Letter of Intent. Normally, you will provide guidance to your legal counsel on what you want the LOI to include and what has been agreed to by both parties. The lawyer then drafts the actual document, and you approve it before sending it over to the seller. Let's now delve into the major components of the LOI.

THE OPENING PARAGRAPHS

The opening of the Letter of Intent serves as a qualitative marketing piece to set up the rest of the document. It is a description of how the two parties came to this point, similar to the opening section of the Pre-LOI Presentation. It contains the strategic rationale for the acquisition, including why you are interested in the prospect and where you see the fit. The opening need not be long but should be substantial enough to serve as a strong reminder of why the deal is taking place. Remember, the opening of the LOI is targeted at more than just the seller and his lawyers. This is the place to speak to those who have significant influence over the seller's decision. As the buyer, you will not be in the room when the seller contemplates this document. The LOI, particularly the opening, needs to be written in your voice, reinforcing the strategic rationale for the acquisition.

A NARROW PRICE RANGE

Although buyers usually prefer not to include price for fear of ramifications later, most sellers want to see a price mentioned in the LOI. If this is the case, I recommend inclusion. The key is to establish a narrow price range. If you believe the business is worth $35 million, then the LOI should propose a price between $34 million and $36 million. If you were to suggest a range between $30 million and $40 million, the seller would remember only the $40 million, while your board will remember only the $30 million!

More important than the price range, though, is a detailed briefing on how you arrived at your numbers. This includes a detailed list of the three major inputs for the initial valuation that we discussed in Chapter 9—any financial documents you've received from the prospect, the information you have acquired in meetings, and any assumptions you've had to make. You can also include charts and graphs to further substantiate your initial offer.

The main purpose of your briefing is to take some of the emotion out of the debate over price. Both sides now have a relatively objective document to work from. Transparency in the math removes much of the mystery from the price negotiations and gives you a solid basis to incorporate any new information. In particular, the assumptions that you include in the LOI place the onus on the seller to provide more accurate data. As new information arises, you can progressively adjust your calculations to arrive at the final price.

BUYING WHAT YOU THINK YOU'RE BUYING

As you know, the acquisition process can be a long one, taking months or even years, and in business, conditions can change quickly. Over this extended period, you want to ensure that the company you started negotiating with is the same one you will receive once the deal is closed. To that end, you need to include in the LOI a metric that provides an objective way to determine that the business is substantially the same at closing as it has been during the negotiations.

The metric I prefer to use here is *net working capital*. The relevant clause typically states that the net working capital is expected to be substantially the same at close as it was at the time the LOI was signed. This prevents the owners from monkeying around with the business for the next six months, or however long it takes to close. For example, they cannot expect the same purchase price if they start taking cash out of the company, or if they've depleted or sold assets, or if they've collected receivables without settling the payables. I have even seen some owners try to give themselves large bonuses just before closing—another practice a net working capital clause can prevent.

STOCK DEAL VS. ASSET DEAL

If, at this point, you've determined whether the sale will be an asset deal or a stock deal, you can also include those details just after your section on price. As the buyer, you should have an idea of which you prefer, particularly since the tax implications could significantly alter what you would really be paying. Figures 11-1 and 11-2 show the basic differences between a stock deal and an asset deal. In a stock deal, you take ownership of the entire company, including all its assets and all its liabilities. In an asset deal, you are acquiring specific components that hold value for you. In Figure 11-1, you can see that the buyer is paying the stockholders, so that the entire company is acquired. In Figure 11-2, you can see that the buyer

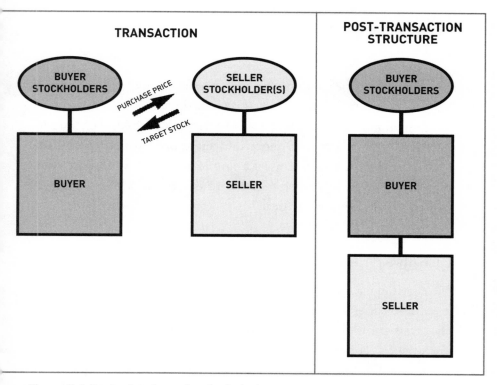

Figure 11-1. Basic structure of a stock deal.

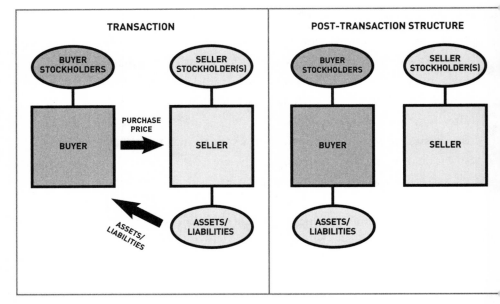

Figure 11-2. Basic structure of an asset deal.

is paying the seller's company for specific assets (and sometimes liabilities), but the company itself remains intact.

Sometimes you may not be able to decide which kind of transaction structure is best until more information is revealed post-LOI. If that is the case, you can insert a simple placeholder sentence reading, "The parties will work together to determine whether this will be an asset deal or a stock deal."

BINDING TERMS AND CONFIDENTIALITY

Most of the clauses in the LOI are nonbinding, meaning that there are no penalties for either party if the deal does not go through or the terms are adjusted once due diligence proper is completed. There are some exceptions, however. The LOI always contains a binding element laying out who is responsible for the various expenses of the transaction process itself.

Another important binding element is confidentiality, and detailed attention must be paid to figuring out who can see which documents and with whom the deal can be discussed. A nondisclosure agreement may have been previously signed, but the LOI can reinforce and strengthen confidentiality. Sellers are often concerned that if the buyers are actual or potential competitors, they may just gather vital information and walk away from the deal. With that in mind, limiting information access to the key players and working through third-party advisers increases the security of the data and puts both sides at ease.

If a seller is particularly anxious, I've gone as far in the LOI as to list who can receive which types of information as well as to require individual nondisclosure agreements for anyone who may touch a potentially confidential document. We have also made use of virtual data rooms where only authorized users can access information. This prevents the e-mailing of large files, which can get stuck in transmission and then be seen by people in IT—a frequent source of leaks.

TIMETABLE UNTIL CLOSING

Next in the Letter of Intent is a timetable for the remainder of the acquisition process. Instead of specific dates, I suggest using time intervals. This is a way to incorporate unavoidable delays that could throw off the whole calendar. For example, it may take more time than you anticipated for the LOI to get signed by the seller, rendering subsequent dates unusable. However, if you establish a time period—such as stating that due diligence will begin fourteen days after the LOI is signed—you can hold to an efficient timetable without being a slave to the calendar.

The timetable also presents an opportunity to manage the seller's expectations. I've seen sellers try to push for a closing date thirty to sixty days after the LOI is signed. This is usually unrealistic. From my experience, 180 days is a more typical time frame for the deal to close. The seller may push back, but you should try to stick to the longer period for the sake of thoroughness and so that all loose ends can be tied up. (See Figure 11-3 for a typical timeline.)

NO-SHOP VS. GO-SHOP

The LOI often establishes a binding exclusivity through a "no-shop" provision. Once you've reached this point, you may want to ensure that the seller cannot try to find a better deal somewhere else. Occasionally, though, I've had buyers include a "go-shop" clause. This gives the seller a certain period of time (usually around fifty days) to see if he can find a better deal. One of the prime reasons to use a go-shop clause is to quell the dissent of minority shareholders who aren't convinced that your deal is the best possible one out there. If, after fifty days, the majority owner comes back and informs them that there was no better deal, the rebellion stops.

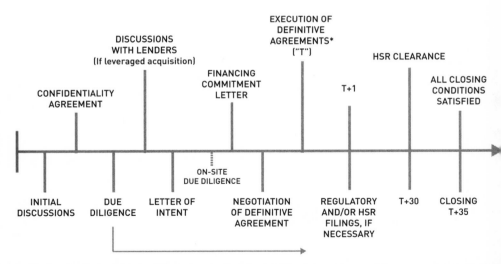

*Transactions not requiring notifications under Hart-Scott-Rodino Act, or other regulatory approval, typically sign and close simultaneously. Closing happens once the transaction is funded.

Figure 11-3. A typical transaction timeline.

ALWAYS, SOMETIMES, NEVER

There are elements the LOI should always include, others it should sometimes include, and a few that it should never include. Here is a summary:

Always

The LOI must include:

- **General valuation (a range of figures), with adjustment mechanisms.** These are to be solidified once all financial information is available.
- **Deal breaker conditions.** This includes items like a substantial change in net working capital.
- **Responsibility for expenses.** This should be a binding clause.
- **Exclusivity or go-shop.** This should be a binding clause.
- **Confidentiality.** This should be a binding clause.
- **Timetable for deal closure.**
- **Tentative thoughts on the transaction structure** (for instance, stock or asset deal). This is not binding, but as discussed above, there needs to be language addressing this even if it hasn't been decided.
- **Flexibility enhancers.** This gives you the flexibility to get out of a deal should the need arise. Examples are phrases such as "Subject to customary agreement" or "Subject to escrow."

Sometimes

The LOI may or may not include the following, at your discretion:

- **Indemnification parameters.** These are "no fault" clauses for the protection of both parties in the event of the collapse of the deal.

- ◆ **Escrow range and terms.**
- ◆ **Survival period of representations and warranties.** This spells out how long the information being given is good for.
- ◆ **Financing arrangements.**
- ◆ **Employment arrangements.** This details who stays and who goes from the seller's staff.
- ◆ **Corporate governance matters.** This states who gets seats on the board of the new company.
- ◆ **Contingencies/conditions to close.** This includes regulatory approvals, access and consents, resolution of pending litigation, or whatever else needs to be resolved for the deal to be complete.

Never

The LOI should never include:

- ◆ **Binding closing obligations.** Again, with the exceptions mentioned, the terms of the LOI should be nonbinding.
- ◆ **Breakup fees payable by the buyer.** The buyer is never monetarily responsible for backing away.
- ◆ **Earnest money deposits.** These are generally never asked for or included, although they are used very, very rarely in the right set of circumstances (e.g., big buyer, small prospect, a first-time seller who is very nervous about the buyer walking away).

Note that the "Sometimes" section contains items that may have been negotiated already or will have to be worked out eventually, but they are included now to reassure the seller. This is particularly true if the seller is concerned about financing and wants to know early on where the money is going to come from.

THE LOI SIGNATURE: A MILESTONE

We've seen in this chapter how the basic structure of the LOI comes together as a short document that provides a jump-start to the rest of the acquisition process. Once you receive a signature on the LOI from the seller, you have reached a significant landmark on the acquisition Roadmap. Even though the LOI contains mostly non-binding elements, it is in effect a gentleman's agreement that the deal will come to a close and that both sides will make a good-faith effort to complete it efficiently. Despite this milestone, the path from the LOI to the purchase agreement is marked with pitfalls. You can allow yourself a moment of relief after the LOI is signed, but you must immediately prepare to bring the deal home—the focus of the next chapter.

CHAPTER 12

GETTING DOWN
TO BUSINESS

WITH THE LETTER OF INTENT signed by both parties, you are now within sight of the finish line. Nevertheless, some major steps remain to complete the acquisition process: due diligence (both on-site and financial), final valuation, drafting the Deal Structure document and Purchase Agreement, and integration planning. While it may be tempting to rush through these steps so you can more quickly reap the benefits of the newly structured company, doing so can be perilous. As I mentioned in the last chapter, it can take up to six months from the signing of the LOI to the closing of the deal.

Due diligence is the most demanding phase of the acquisition process. You are zeroing in from a 10,000-foot view of the deal to a microscopic examination of every facet. As the saying goes, the devil is in the details, and during due diligence, your objective is to identify anything that could fundamentally change your understanding of the company you thought you were buying when you signed the LOI.

Throughout this final phase, you must maintain your role of leadership in the acquisition process. As you approach harbor, it is still your duty to steer the ship. This is a time when you need to remain cautious about lawyers and other experts taking over the process. While these advisers are both necessary and helpful, it is still your deal—not theirs. For example, a lawyer's job is to attempt to eliminate risk. However, an acquisition inherently carries risk that can never be eliminated. In this final phase, your main focus is to *reduce* that risk, while understanding that you cannot be completely free of it.

In this chapter, we look at due diligence in a new way—as an opportunity rather than a chore. With this new outlook in mind, we explore how best to find and sort the information that is gathered, as well as how to work with the seller to ensure that you are buying what you think you are buying. We also look at the more technical side of due diligence—the financial and legal aspects that are essential to crossing the t's and dotting the i's on any deal—along with the final valuation. We finish by examining the actual document that seals the deal, the Purchase Agreement, leaving integration planning for the next chapter.

DUE DILIGENCE: CONVENTIONAL THINKING VS. NEW THINKING

Traditionally, after the LOI is signed, an army of lawyers and accountants descend upon the seller (or meet in a secret location), pore through financials and company records, and possibly conduct an interview or two with top executives. They uncover the significant risks, and then the deal is renegotiated based on their findings. Apart from risk analysis and allocation, the traditional functions of due diligence in company acquisitions have included:

→ **Evaluating Strengths and Weaknesses.** With the release of more detailed information, you are getting your most in-depth look at the seller so you can seize the opportunity to evaluate the company's true strengths and weaknesses, both financially (for example, most profitable products) and operationally (for example, least efficient divisions).

◆ **Uncovering Liabilities.** Hidden problems could prevent you from realizing the true synergy created by the soon-to-be-formed company, such as issues with past litigation, a questionable patent, or an aging piece of equipment.

◆ **Renegotiating Based on Findings.** If you get your first in-depth look at the books and discover that not everything is as it seemed, you will need to renegotiate the monetary aspect of the deal equation.

◆ **Checking the Boxes and Filling in the Blanks.** The overall purpose of due diligence is to ensure that there are no surprises or "gotchas" when the transaction is completed.

All of these functions remain perfectly valid. However, I have found that the conventional approach to due diligence is largely inadequate. Too often, those responsible merely focus on completing a checklist that has been handed to them. Just as the Roadmap is a new way to think about the acquisition process as a whole, I advocate new thinking on due diligence.

The first step is to take a different view on when it starts. Due diligence should begin well before the LOI is signed. In fact, it should be part of your work from the beginning of the entire acquisition process—way back when you develop your initial strategic plan.

From the moment you lay out your plan and develop your acquisition criteria, you should be gathering information along functional lines to see how well what you discover matches your objectives. All the research you put into market and prospect selection is really part of your due diligence. So what does this say about the final phase, the one that is normally characterized as "due diligence"? Very simply, once the LOI is signed, you should be confirming—not learning. Your prior research should have been so thorough that the new data you receive should provide support for what you had already discovered rather than reveal important new information. There should be few if any surprises after the signatures have dried on the LOI.

Another valuable way to think about due diligence is to see the process as an aspect of integration planning. The details you discover will suggest valuable new ways to combine the acquired entity with your company. If due diligence is the gathering of information, integration is the implementation of what you discover. The two processes fit hand in glove.

As you evaluate the strengths and weaknesses of the target company, you should be on the lookout not only for problems but also for profitable enhancements to the newly formed entity. For instance, you may discover inefficiencies in a particular division that are leading to reduced output. Correcting this once the deal closes could make a rapid contribution to the bottom line.

As well as watching for red flags, you can be scanning the company for hidden assets, such as a talented manager or other employee. Throughout due diligence, you should be on the lookout for "stars"—employees who quickly grasp the rationale and value of the merger, once they are informed about it. For instance, if you are buying a company to open up your product to new geographic markets, an experienced sales manager who knows the region can be an extremely valuable resource.

The Three Buckets of Critical Information

This new approach to due diligence calls on you to see information gathering in terms of the opportunities that it offers, not just the negatives. The opportunities for integration success, for finding stars, even for crafting a unique Deal Structure—all of these focus your attention on creating an outcome that matches the strategic rationale for acquisition that you started with.

This forward-looking focus during due diligence will prevent you from getting bogged down in the minutiae that so often besets the process. If you adopt the approach that you are confirming rather than learning through this post-LOI period, then you will actually be solidifying the strategic rationale for the acquisition. Even though you are now examining the acquisition through a microscope, what you are discovering should always be considered in terms of your overall business objectives.

I like to reinforce this idea with my clients in a meeting with the buyer's team the night before on-site due diligence begins at the seller's facilities. I advise them that their responsibility is to ensure that the new company that emerges from the acquisition will be the best it can be. This encourages them to identify star employees and best practices in the seller's organization so that management can figure out a way to keep the top players on board and integrate the optimum practices. Such an approach can have challenging implications. For example, if you find a manager in the seller's organization who does a better job than her counterpart in your own organization, there should be no assumption that it is your employee who will remain.

At the first due diligence team meeting, we have the lead person from each functional area deliver a short verbal report on his focus for the next day. This keeps interaction between the functional groups high and avoids information silos. I suggest having the reports given verbally because this encourages clear and succinct thinking. At the end of each day on-site, you should hold a similar meeting, with verbal reports on the day's findings from all the team leaders describing what they've learned, what they don't understand, and what they still need to find out. Again, a verbal report helps keep the speaker on the point while allowing the team to collaborate on how best to use the findings and how to gather the information still needed.

With all of this in mind, you need a way to organize the fresh information you uncover that encourages the team to look beyond

196 BUILD THE DEAL

the negatives. At my firm, we place every new discovery in one of three color-coded "buckets":

1. **Red Bucket: Deal Changers.** This is information that materially alters what you thought you were buying. These are the true surprises, and they can have a serious effect on the deal, such as a previously unknown pending court case on a key technology or a likely decline in revenue.

2. **Yellow Bucket: Acceptable Risks.** These are new items that you discover about the seller that you can live with but can't ignore. For example, a new product from the seller may not be ready to go to market for a year when you expected only a six-month wait. You would probably not cancel the deal because of this, but it's still something you will have to take into account and alter your plans accordingly.

3. **Green Bucket: Integration Opportunities.** This is information that adds value and synergies to the deal, usually in the form of cost savings or revenue growth. A typical example occurs in the purchasing department, where the seller may be paying a significant percentage more than the buyer because he is not ordering in the volume necessary to reach price breaks.

The bucket method will help you to contain everyone's emotions in the process. With closing in sight and your team of experts poring over the seller, tensions can begin to escalate. No individual likes to be nitpicked, and the same goes for companies. By handling new information with a larger focus on your strategic objective, you can avoid at least some of these negative effects. If you come across a piece of data that belongs in the red "Deal Changer" bucket, bring it back to the seller with clear reasons for your concern and a straightforward explanation of *how* you think it changes the deal. Give the seller a chance to explain the issue and hold a constructive discussion on possible solutions.

Who Does Due Diligence?

The role of the Acquisition Coordinator is to continue to steer the ship and always keep a strategic focus, but there are several others involved in due diligence. As well as the outside experts—lawyers, valuation consultants, and accountants—most of your A-Team shares responsibility for the process. Assuming your acquisition team includes members from all the functional areas of your business, each of those individuals should head up the due diligence for his area.

Your third-party adviser can play a valuable role in recommending experts and organizing your A-Team to take on its due diligence responsibilities. However, I advise against ceding too much control to your outside adviser. It is imperative that you maintain leadership and stay involved. That said, the adviser can help guide you through the process and provide a sounding board for any concerns you may have.

After you've organized your due diligence team along functional lines (see Figure 12-1), have the head of each functional area create a list of questions for his counterpart on the seller's side. The inspiration for these questions should be your original prospect criteria. For example, the sales member of the diligence team may request all of the performance figures for the seller's sales team, while the head of the manufacturing team will want a list of all the capital equipment in the plant.

The Acquisition Coordinator should review each functional area's list, edit it for relevance, and make sure that nothing important is missing. She should then create a single comprehensive list of questions and document requests to hand over to the seller. You can see from this that I strongly advocate presenting all your questions to the seller together. If you deliver multiple lists of questions spread over several weeks, you risk killing the seller with paper cuts and losing track of which information you have and which you still need. Our approach also helps to avoid suspicion among the seller's

SALES & MARKETING	PRODUCTS/ OPERATIONS	HR/ MANAGEMENT	SUPPLIER	LEGAL	SHAREHOLDER AND STRUCTURE	ADDITIONAL ISSUES
High concentration of sales in one customer or one salesperson	Current & expected capacity	Personal references, background checks	Critical raw materials	Past litigation hidden	Family members of the Target's management	Environmental
Geography	High skill levels	Training & education policies; invest in employees?	Favorable pricing terms	Continuity of officers	Future commitments of stockholders	Health & safety
Product line	Obsolete equipment	Unions in place?	Supply commitments	Lack of/sloppy corporate records	Stock/asset purchase issues	Intellectual property
Sales territory	Certifications required	Succession planning	Favorable credit terms	Rep & warranty issues	Earnout issues	Information technology
Noncompetes	State of manufacturing	Keeping key players	Transfer of contracts	Subchapter S conversions	Tax implications	
Retaining key salespeople	Critical employees & institutional knowledge	Lack of records	Purchasing department audit			
	Preventative maintenance/ replacement policy	Unfair hiring practices	Decision process			
	Quality program	Liability of terminated employees				
		Contracts				
		Benefits				

Figure 12-1. Typical data in functional due diligence.

employees that would certainly be raised if they were constantly being asked for more and more information.

As documents are handed over to you, meticulously track them so their return is easily facilitated. Remember, you are now dealing with much more sensitive material and the seller expects it to remain confidential. The most common way that information is exchanged today is through virtual data rooms (VDRs). These allow documents to be uploaded and stored online securely, with access limited to the proper users. When someone views a document, the event is recorded with the date, time, and how long he viewed it. In addition to the extra security afforded by VDRs, they save tremendously on printing and shipping costs.

As each functional area sorts through the information it receives, you will begin to see answers to the questions you have collected on the comprehensive list. I recommend a weekly meeting between the heads of the functional areas and the Acquisition Coordinator to assess progress, check off the comprehensive question list, and—above all—avoid information silos. Inevitably, there will be follow-up questions. Again, for the sake of efficiency and courtesy, gather all the follow-ups and present one list to the prospect.

Extracting the Best Information

There are a handful of simple questions that can uncover rich seams of information about the seller's company. These "tricks of the trade" have served me well over the years in gaining extra insight into the seller's world.

◆ **Read the seller's board minutes.** If you know what the board has recently discussed, you will catch a glimpse of the most pressing issues facing the company. You will also likely see how those issues were resolved—or not—over a period of time.

◆ **Request organizational charts.** Have each of your functional area leaders ask her counterpart on the seller's side to draw the organizational chart for the whole company. How the seller's executives perceive the structure of the company can tell you how the chain of command works in reality. I like to do this in a casual environment, away from the office, so that the executives cannot simply hand over the printed corporate chart.

◆ **Map out the work flow process from sales to invoice.** Again, there may be varying perceptions of what really happens, and you can compare these viewpoints with the picture you got from the CEO to ensure that everyone is on the same page.

◆ **Perform background checks, including credit checks, on key individuals.** You may think you know whom you are getting into business with, but sometimes (albeit rarely), you will discover a skeleton that can make you think twice.

Regarding background checks, in one instance, we found a controller who had filed for bankruptcy—twice. This was not exactly the type of person you want controlling the books, so his release was part of the final acquisition agreement. In addition, graft happens, not only in the finance departments. I've actually found that dishonesty occurs most often in purchasing. We were once looking at a manufacturing prospect in the cable industry with a purchasing manager I'll call "Perry." It was clear that Perry's lifestyle—the custom-tailored suits, the $70,000 SUV—did not match the salary we knew he was being paid. After first looking at his real estate records, we discreetly drove past his house and saw spools of high-priced cable in his side yard. Perry was buying extra cable with company funds and then selling it on the side and pocketing the cash. Obviously, his services were no longer required and the authorities were alerted.

Perhaps the biggest secret to due diligence is knowing when to stop. This process can go on forever if you let it. You can constantly ask for more and more information from the seller, who may continue to provide it, but at some point the endless pursuit of data causes acrimony on both sides. That is why I recommend a single, comprehensive list of initial questions and then one list of follow-ups. While the information you want can be detailed, it should always be relevant to the deal. As before, if you keep your strategic purpose in mind, you can be both thorough and efficient.

Negotiating the Red Bucket Items

Once you have a complete sense of the red bucket (deal-changing) items, you will need to negotiate new terms with the seller, revising the preliminary deal you agreed upon. Again, I recommend negotiating these items all together—not in series.

When it comes to the red bucket items, there are a number of ways to protect yourself as the buyer, some more impactful than others. These include:

- Ask the seller to fix the problem and continue in good faith.
- Insist upon indemnification so the seller is legally bound to cover the costs if the problem materializes.
- Institute holdbacks, where a certain amount of the payment price is withheld to cover the specific issue of concern.
- Request that funds be held in escrow to cover the problem and other potential contingencies.
- Offer less money for the business.

Negotiation of the red bucket items is one of those tougher tasks in which you may want to involve your third-party adviser. He can protect the relationship between buyer and seller, acting as a marriage counselor resolving potential points of conflict. You can present your adviser with the problem and ask him to investigate and develop possible solutions to present to the seller. Having taken this role in numerous deals, I know the importance firsthand of taking the emotion out of the process at this delicate stage.

Financial Due Diligence

The functional due diligence that you undertake with your A-Team is complemented by financial due diligence of the seller's books, usually conducted by expert accountants who specialize in this area. While you can allow your own in-house accountants to perform this work, I caution against it. The intricacies of financial due diligence are different from the everyday accounting that takes place in most businesses. However, it is important that you understand the overall process and the general areas of analysis. Figure 12-2 shows the chart I use to explain key elements of financial due diligence to my clients.

Financial due diligence involves more than making sure the books are up to snuff, essential though this is. It also has a strategic purpose. By looking at such items as the concentration of the seller's accounts receivable, current inventory, and liability-related issues,

ASSET DOCUMENTATION	LIABILITIES & EQUITY	INVISIBLE RISKS	REVENUES	EXPENSES
Cash/cash flow bank records	Trade payables	Off-balance sheet liabilities	Revenues	Expenses
Trade receivables	Supplier contracts	Contingent liabilities (lawsuits, product liability)	Client contracts	Supplier contracts
Client contracts & customer lists	Outstanding and paid invoices, payment terms	Environmental liabilities	Bank statements	Bank statements
Accounts aging	Non-invoiced payables	Contested or unproven title (land)	Audited financial statements	Audited finanical statements
Accounts receivable	Tax records and liabilities due	Pension liabilities	Product and price lists	Profitability analyses
Inventories	Credit	Capitalized leases	Market segmentation analyses	Warranty claims, log of complaints
Inventory list & aging	Banks or other creditors		Accounting treatment issues	Record of performance problems
Latest physical inventory report	Equity		Recognition (are discounts an expense or simply left out of revenue for example)	Tax returns and statements
Other receivables - loan contracts and repayment history	Articles of incorporation		When does revenue recognition occur?	Accounting treatment issues
Tax records and correspondence	Shareholder agreements and other documentation		Other revenues	Recognition (capitalized or expensed)
Intangible assets	Audited financial statements		Recurring or onetime?	Timing of events (when does expense recognition occur?)
Patents, copyright and trademarks			Do revenues reflect the ability of the business to perform in the future?	Restatements, depreciation, LIFO vs. FIFO
Employment or similar contracts with key employees				
Fixed assets, legal title & leasing contracts				

Figure 12-2. Typical balance sheet data in financial due diligence.

you can confirm your criteria-driven picture of the company and ensure that it matches your strategic outcomes.

What to Do with the Lawyers

Just as you need an accountant experienced in financial due diligence, you want a lawyer at your side who specializes in acquisitions. Previously, I remarked that I always hope the seller has a lawyer who "speaks M&A." When it comes to due diligence and crafting the deal structure, this point holds equally true for you. Just as you wouldn't see a podiatrist for a heart problem, you don't want a criminal attorney handling your company acquisitions. A good M&A lawyer will best know how to handle questions of past, current, and future litigation, as well as issues of representation and warranty.

As we know, attorneys by nature seek to eliminate risk in any negotiation. And as we also know, this is a quixotic pursuit—risk is an inherent component of any acquisition. If you let the lawyers lead the due diligence process, it may never finish. Lawyers are essential at this stage, but they must be kept on a short leash.

FINAL VALUATION

We've established that due diligence allows you to confirm your assumptions about each functional area of the prospect company, based on information you have gathered since the beginning. In the same way, it also enables you to solidify the numbers behind your valuation of the company. With fuller access to the seller's books, you will be able to plug new numbers into the methods you used for your initial valuation to arrive at more accurate figures.

Even with more precise numbers, valuation still has the potential to be a stressful exercise where emotions run high. You can mitigate some of this by turning to an independent valuation expert. This will demonstrate that you are not trying to force an unfair number into the deal, and it can also provide the seller with a much needed reality check. You and the seller can split the cost of the expert so no bias is perceived. The independent expert should have the skills to talk the seller through the valuation process if the seller is uneducated or nervous. This is another step that can remove some of the emotion from the final stages and ease everyone toward a speedier conclusion.

DRAFTING THE DEAL STRUCTURE DOCUMENT AND PURCHASE AGREEMENT

Once due diligence is complete, you will finalize the Deal Structure with the seller in a written document. This often takes the form of a graphic representation of the deal and may present a choice of alternative possible deal structures. Adding the new information that you have gathered, along with your revised valuation, to what has been previously negotiated, you will determine the final equation that will persuade the seller to sign on the dotted line.

The Deal Structure document comprises three major components:

1. **Legal Structure.** This includes the method: stock purchase, asset purchase, or a merger. It also defines what happens with each functional area once the deal is complete. Finally, it contains all of the negotiated representations and warranties, such as the net working capital clause discussed in the previous chapter.

2. **Financial.** This not only specifies the price you are going to pay for the company but also earnouts and responsibilities for any tax implications.

3. **The Rest of the Equation.** The Deal Structure contains all the other issues that are important to the seller, such as continued employment, car or similar perks, and involvement in the community. These are the tradables that you have used to entice the prospect and complete the seller's equation.

The Deal Structure document goes into the Purchase Agreement, the actual legal document that both parties will sign. The agreement can vary slightly depending on whether the deal is a stock purchase or an asset purchase. Asset Purchase Agreements are usually much more detailed because they must list every individual asset that is changing hands as part of the deal.

Typically, a Purchase Agreement breaks down into the following sections:

- **Definitions.** Clarifies terms used in the remainder of the document.

- **Sale and Purchase.** Includes the purchase price while specifying what is actually being bought or sold.

- **Representations and Warranties.** Can be divided into a section for the seller and a section for the buyer; these are what the buyer and seller claim as the underlying facts of the contract.

- **Indemnification.** Penalizes the buyer or the seller for loss or damages sustained as a result of the deal.

- **Closing.** What needs to happen for the deal to close, such as the removal of personal items (such as a vehicle) from the business premises.

- **Postclosing Matters.** Clauses that handle matters that may arise after closing; for example, the sellers may have to hold information related to their company confidential for an extended period of time.

At this stage, you are also making arrangements for funding the deal. You may have to present documentation to the seller about where the financing will come from and how the money will be transferred.

CLOSING THE DEAL

With due diligence performed, the final Deal Structure worked out, the financing secured, and the Purchase Agreement drafted, there are two final steps to complete the acquisition: the signing, and throwing a big party! All of your hard work has come to fruition and you are now the proud owner of a new, stronger company.

However, your job is not over. In fact, one of the most crucial phases of the entire acquisition process remains: integration. Planning and implementing the integration of the two formerly separate companies has a huge impact on the success of the acquisition. This is the focus of the next chapter.

CHAPTER 13

INTEGRATION: AN END AND A NEW BEGINNING

THE CLOSING OF AN acquisition deal is the fruition of months—even years—of hard work. It's no secret, though, that a whole new round of work begins the moment the ink dries on that prized contract. The integration of two companies is a major operation that requires skill, diligence, and patience. We may be at the end of the buying process, but we are standing at the threshold of a new episode—the marriage of two entities, each with its own history, capabilities, weaknesses, and culture.

In this chapter, I can't hope to cover every aspect of integration, a subject of massive complexity. What we will do here is discuss how to prepare for integration throughout the acquisition process, as well as briefly address two of the biggest issues raised by integration: communication and culture. I also advocate for the use of secondment as an effective way to smooth the transition from two companies into one. Most important, I will place these aspects in the context of your overall acquisition strategy.

Needless to say, advance planning is critical to integration success. In fact, it's my belief that planning for integration begins when due diligence begins—way back at the start of the entire acquisition process. As I have emphasized, the two go hand in glove: Due diligence is the information gathering, while integration is the implementation, so the overall shape of the union should be mapped out well ahead of time as data and insights are being collected.

THE SECRET TO INTEGRATION SUCCESS

There are countless books on how to effectively integrate two companies after an acquisition. Some stress communication, while others put the emphasis on culture. While both concepts are important, neither is the key to integration success. In my experience, the single best thing you can do to ensure a smooth integration is to *buy the right company*.

This may seem self-evident, but in many cases the choice of target is the hidden source of endless integration problems. If you've bought the wrong company, no amount of force or ingenuity can squeeze a square peg into a round hole. We have established that "the right company" means a company that serves a single, well-defined strategic purpose. Experience shows that integration is infinitely easier when the buyer and the seller are aligned on the strategic rationale for the combination. Throughout the entire acquisition process, from market and prospect research through negotiations and due diligence, you have been looking for the characteristics, opportunities, resources, people, and culture that will make an ideal fit with your own enterprise. Assuming you have done that right, it is reasonable to expect a relatively happy union.

How Much Should You Integrate?

The degree of integration you engineer will vary according to your strategic purpose. You may want to leave the seller mostly alone, happy to let a successful business continue down its own path with some periodic guidance from above. You could go a step further and combine some of the back office functions for the sake of efficiency, while staying mostly hands-off with the rest of the business. For example, if you are buying a supplier that has served you well in the past, you may integrate HR or accounting but leave the operations side alone.

A greater amount of integration could be demanded if you are acquiring a competitor to absorb that enterprise's market share, such as a national restaurant chain that is buying up a small regional competitor. Here, nearly every aspect of the acquired entity has to change, from the operations to the menu to the employees' uniforms.

Reverse Integration

Integration need not be a one-way street, with only the buyer bringing her systems or culture to the newly acquired company. The seller may have assets or characteristics that will benefit the buyer (see Figure 13-1). Remember that part of our Roadmap approach is

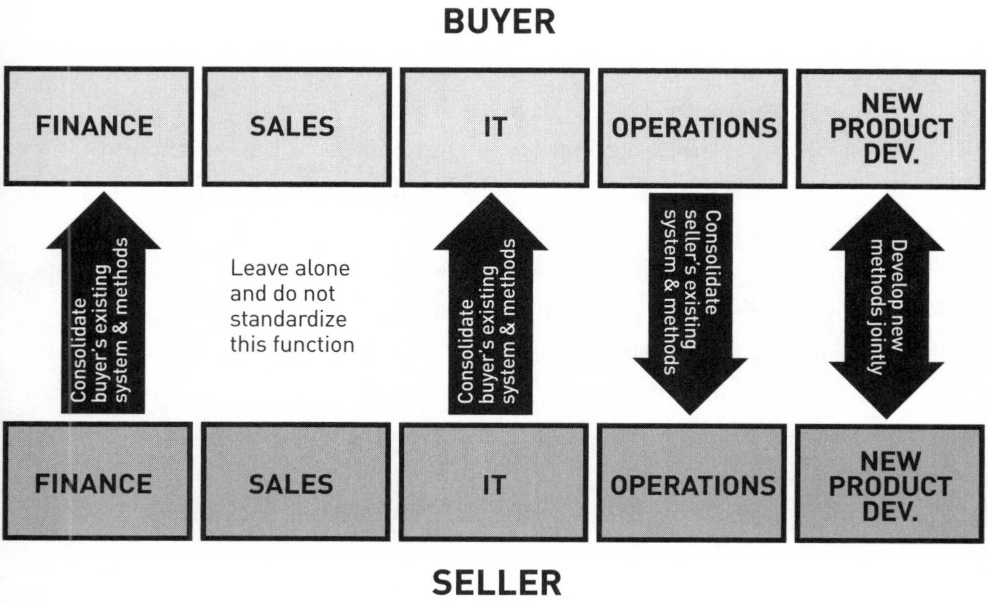

Figure 13-1. Examples of how integration works both ways.

to look for integration opportunities while conducting due diligence. That would include identifying practices of the seller that you may want to bring back to your own company. These practices, such as having a unique sales team structure that considerably increased the bottom line, may even be the reason you were attracted to the seller in the first place. It would make sense to incorporate that winning structure into your own sales process now that you are part of the same organization.

The 100-Day Plan

Whatever level of integration is appropriate to your strategic rationale, you need a precise plan to carry it through. I recommend creating a 100-Day Plan that addresses two questions: Where do we begin? And what do we want the new company to look like after the first 100 days?

Once a merger is announced, employees from both the buyer and the seller naturally expect changes to occur. If you move quickly in the first 100 days, this anticipation can soften the impact of the changes you implement. If you dawdle, you are likely to meet more resistance as employees go back to business as usual. Of course, integration may not be complete within 100 days, but by then you should be well on your way to realizing the synergies you expected from the acquisition.

Beginnings are powerful. What you do on Day One of the integration program has practical implications for the entire process. For example, one of the biggest questions you are likely to face is what to do about the payroll system. Employees rightly expect to get paid without interruption, on time, and in the correct amount. If you decide to consolidate accounting departments, there is potential for logistical confusion as the new employees are brought into the system.

Accounting and human resources are particularly vulnerable functions in the early stages, depending on the level of integration desired. In addition to payroll issues, the financial team needs to quickly decide how accounts receivable and accounts payable are handled. HR may face a huge new volume of work—especially in an asset deal, where the seller's employees essentially need to be re-hired. Health insurance, retirement plans, sick days, and more all need to be accounted for.

A written integration plan is essential, and swift execution of your plan will heighten its chances of success within the new organization. Even some of the simplest details can get overlooked on Day One. There's a painful historical lesson to be learned from the acquisition of Sovran Bank by NationsBank back in 1991. At the time of the acquisition, there was a huge PR effort to trump the transition to the NationsBank brand. On Day One, though, some Sovran Bank locations were still Sovran Bank—because someone had forgotten to order the new NationsBank signs!

It makes sense to organize integration by functional area, just as you organized due diligence. Your acquisition team, which has representatives from each area of the business, should be charged with building and implementing the integration plan. They can identify the urgent actions that must be taken on Day One, or shortly thereafter. They should also have a vision for how their departments should look after 100 days.

When I'm consulting on integration, I use an Integration Checklist detailing the issues each functional area needs to think about. Figure 13-2 provides a summary table of this checklist.

A seamless integration naturally supports the employees of the new company, but it also speaks well to your suppliers and customers. By showing them that you are able to handle the transition smoothly, you are building their confidence in the new company. Note, for instance, that the Integration Checklist in Figure 13-2 includes points you may need to negotiate with your suppliers.

It's Not About More Communication

Communication is often promoted as the key to integration success. The quality of communication is certainly important: You need to

OPERATIONS	FINANCE & ACCT.	IT SYSTEMS	SALES & MKTG.	SUPPLIERS
Capacity utilization	Payroll	System platforms	Pricing strategies	Critical inputs
Automation vs. manual	Financial reporting & controls	Hidden "black magic" experts	Branding	Favorable pricing terms
Critical employees & institutional knowledge	Outsourcing vs. captive	Scalability	Hiring & training	Supply commitments
Equipment compatibility	Capital expenditure procedures	Compatibility	Sales territory redundancies	Favorable credit terms
State of manufacturing processes	State of the financials		Distribution	Transfer of contracts
Certifications required	Working capital challenges		Compensation plans	

Figure 13-2. Integration Checklist organized along functional lines.

maintain honesty and credibility as you bring the two entities together. However, it is misguided to believe that increasing the *quantity* of communication facilitates the process. Rather than holding dozens of meetings and sending hundreds of e-mails, it is more effective to have your actions demonstrate your intent.

Communication difficulties inevitably occur during the integration process. Mergers often cause the level of trust in a company to decline because employees are uncertain about their future. As a result, people play their cards closer to their chest and everyone begins to receive less dependable information (or no information at all). Rumors then fill the vacuum.

Despite your best efforts, you can never completely eliminate the uncertainty that goes with integration. Your main objective should be to minimize that uncertainty, particularly for issues that directly impact employees. If, say, you plan to change something sensitive, like vacation policy, you need to candidly and concisely explain to employees the why, when, and how of the change. If you dance around an issue or deliver half-truths, you will lose credibility and employee morale will be severely damaged.

I often recommend setting up a toll-free hotline that enables employees to anonymously vent their frustrations and ask about rumors. Another approach is to create a blog to disseminate information and allow employees to comment. Both of these solutions allow management to know what employees are concerned about and to respond quickly.

A succinct way to communicate with employees on both sides of the integration process is to publish and distribute your 100-Day Plan. That literally puts everyone on the same page and tells them what will be happening after the merger and what is expected of them.

CULTURAL INTEGRATION

A vitally important but sometimes overlooked aspect of integration is the merging of the two company cultures. Culture can encompass anything from dress code to workplace hours to who pays for the coffee in the employee lounge. How those practices change can have a significant impact on the attitude of employees in the new company. What will make the difference here is a systematic approach to cultural integration.

The process begins by taking a look at your own company and then comparing key aspects with the acquired entity. Any measurement of culture is bound to be ambiguous, so my clients use a Culture Assessment Survey to bring some objectivity to the process. By this stage, you should already have a strong instinct for the seller's culture. Through your company research and due diligence, you have identified many of the seller's core values. You've also learned a lot from your interactions during negotiations. Did they respond quickly to inquiries? Were they on time to meetings, or did they always rush in a few minutes late? You can gain further insight by speaking directly with select employees of the seller and to their suppliers and customers.

The Culture Assessment Survey takes the discovery process one step further. It simply asks you to assess where your company stands between two opposite cultural philosophies. Figure 13-3 gives an example of the survey and some of the cultural characteristics we try to get a handle on. It's best to ask each level—shareholders, executives, managers, and staff—to rank the items on a scale of 1–5. They note "1" if they strongly agree with the philosophy on the left and "5" if they strongly agree with the philosophy on the right. The important insights appear when there are differences among the four levels; for example, shareholders' consensus is "1" for a topic while staff indicate "5" for the same topic.

Your acquisition team should first complete the survey to identify the essential characteristics of your own company culture. The A-Team can then share the survey with their counterparts from the seller. This simple exercise helps you to see, as objectively as possible, what it will take to bring the two cultures into harmony. Let's say your A-Team members reveal that your organization relies mostly on written communication, while their counterparts indicate that they mostly communicate verbally. In this case, you may have to provide guidelines on what kind of communication is to be conducted by memo or e-mail, and when a phone call or face-to-face meeting is necessary.

As with every aspect of this process, the degree of cultural integration depends on why you bought the target in the first place. Suppose that a traditional corporation were to buy a software start-up founded by a couple of twenty-somethings. The start-up has been picked because its young team is smart, hardworking, and innovative—and they have a flagship product that is ready to take off, with similar products in the pipeline. The start-up's culture allows for jeans and tee-shirts in the office and encourages employees to work from home two days a week. The buyer, meanwhile, jealously guards its traditional workplace values: shirts and ties, and

	ALWAYS 1	MOST OF THE TIME 2	ASPECTS OF BOTH 3	MOST OF THE TIME 4	ALWAYS 5	
Centralized Decisions						Dispersed Decisions
Quick Decision Making						Deliberate Decision Making
Short-Term Focus						Long-Term Focus
Risk Taker						Risk Avoidance
Confrontational						Avoid Conflict
Results-Focused						Process-Focused
Performance Measured Often						Performance Measured Sporadically
People Held Accountable						Lack of Accountability
Work Across Organization						Stay in Silos
Low Political Climate						High Political Climate
Open Communications						Cautious Communications
Speedy Communications						Slow Communications
Verbal Communications						Written Communications
Change Discouraged						Change Encouraged

Figure 13-3. Culture Assessment Survey.

fixed office hours. Given the reason for the purchase, it is probably in its interests not to tamper with the start-up's culture as this may dampen its creative spirit. At the opposite end of the scale, when a company like Marriott buys a privately owned hotel for its attractive location, the newly acquired company must change its entire culture so that employees create a consistent atmosphere and customer experience in keeping with the global brand.

BRAND INTEGRATION

A closely related concern is branding, which raises a number of key decisions as you combine the two companies. The brand can be seen as the outward-facing aspect of the company culture. At its heart, the brand is a promise that customers can depend on, rooted in a strong and simple brand concept, a distinct "brand personality," and a recognizable set of values. This promise is projected by the company name, logo, and visual imagery.

When you acquire a new company, you face several options. You can erase your acquisition's brand and simply subsume it under your own brand. This is the obvious step if you are buying a former competitor or if the acquired brand has little market value. Another alternative is to maintain the existing brand in parallel with your own—in which case, you may choose to mark it as a subordinate to your brand ("A division of the X Group"). Finally, in rare cases, you might discard both of the original brands and create a new joint brand.

It makes excellent sense to maintain the seller's brand when it has a well-defined meaning to customers. For example, Avis retained the Budget brand when it acquired the lower-end rental car business. In many airports, it's obvious the two belong to one company, but the brand promise of Budget is all about price, while the brand promise of Avis is more about service. Consumers respond accordingly.

There can be situations where you do not know for sure how

much equity there is in the brand you have acquired. In that case, you may decide to invest in some systematic market research prior to making a decision about the fate of the brand.

The consolidation of major airlines has provided some instructive examples of brand integration. When Continental and United combined, the name of one company was retained and the logo of the other. This meant that both companies could draw on their existing legacy in the marketplace and partially appease the feelings of employees, who tend to develop a strong loyalty to their own company brand.

The airline industry has also demonstrated the problems companies can have with this issue. On a recent flight, I noticed a US Airways logo on the outside of the plane while the America West logo appeared inside on the seat cushions—more than three years after the merger of the two airlines. Although these are minor details, they speak loudly to the complications that often result from brand integration.

The lesson here is that once a firm decision has been made about the brand, it needs to be executed thoroughly and swiftly across the entire gamut of applications. Every touch point with the market must be considered, from business cards to vehicle livery to how the phone is answered. For this exercise, it is important to designate an acquisition team member with sufficient authority and organizational skill to carry the process through to completion.

The rebranding of a company often raises anxiety, not just among employees but also among senior executives. All of them are likely to see only the loss of a name and identity they have been attached to, and they will tend to fear the worst in market reaction. The key to remember here is that, when approached in the right way, a change of brand can be a hugely positive PR opportunity. By installing a new brand, you are effectively delivering a new promise to the market, and that promise can be proclaimed positively and assertively.

SECONDMENT: EMBEDDED INTERPRETERS

I have found that the best way to get a handle on different cultures is through the use of secondment. This involves taking a few people out of the company that you have acquired and placing them in equivalent roles in your own organization. At the same time, you move a handful of people out of your workplace and plug them into the newly acquired company. Usually, this involves at least three people from each side, representing the sales, accounting, and operations departments. Of course, as appropriate, you may add individuals from other functional areas, but do not deploy fewer than three people. I have seen some companies exchange only one person with less than successful results. There is simply too much to learn and communicate for one person to handle, and valuable opportunities can be missed.

These embedded representatives serve as interpreters for their new colleagues concerning the culture they've come from. Choosing the right people for this job takes some skill. It's usually best to select mid-level employees who have enthusiastically embraced their organization's DNA. These dedicated staff members understand the company's culture and processes and can easily share them with their new partners. The move need not be permanent but should last for at least six months—enough time to get everyone up to speed and make the key adjustments that will realize the maximum synergies.

One purpose of secondment is to get a sense of what matters most to the seller's employees, both inside and outside the workplace. I had a client who bought a company in rural Pennsylvania. He discovered that the company traditionally closed its doors for the first week of deer-hunting season. Naturally, he wasn't too thrilled to discover that his new division shut down for a week every year, but his seconded employees warned him that if he took away this privilege, there would be a serious drop in productivity—due both to resentment and the number of people calling in sick during the first week of hunting season!

Secondment also allows the embedded staff to identify hidden problems and bring them up to management. An employee from one of my clients noticed that the organization he was seconded to had made an investment in brand new computers but had retained ancient monitors, keyboards, and other accessories. He took this information back to his superiors, and they decided to invest in peripherals to match the new hardware. It was a simple upgrade, but one that showed employees in the new organization that management was paying attention to detail.

Another area where secondment frequently proves useful is in the financial operations of the acquired company. Some smaller businesses may not have the resources for optimum controls on their books, and everything runs through a single controller. It's the kind of detail that might have escaped you even during due diligence, but seconding an employee from your accounting department will quickly reveal how effective controls are and what needs to be fixed.

READY TO BUY AGAIN

If buying the right company is the key to integration success, then the 100-Day Plan and the use of secondment are both valuable ways to smooth the path to a successful union. However, in even the most ideal circumstances, integration is by nature a time of upheaval because it brings changes and uncertainty to two organizations that must each make adjustments to accommodate the other. As with every aspect of the Roadmap approach, the clearer your focus on the overall strategic objective, the easier your journey through integration will prove.

Each company you buy provides an extraordinary real-world education in the acquisition process, and the knowledge you gain becomes an asset in itself, one you should leverage to the maximum. As soon as you begin the integration stage with the company you bought, you are positioned to plan your next acquisition. The second time around is easier than the first because of the rich knowledge resources now at your disposal—strategy, market research, target research, and negotiating experience.

The Roadmap process has been developed through many years of active experience helping clients buy companies of all shapes and sizes. My hope is that with these powerful tools in your hands, you will experience acquisition not as a once-in-a-lifetime adventure but as an integral part of your growth strategy. You may then discover, as so many of my clients have, that a well-managed acquisition can be the royal road to realizing your business dreams.

EXECUTIVE SUMMARY: THE TOP TEN LESSONS

I WANT TO LEAVE YOU with my Top Ten guiding principles for making a successful acquisition. I hope that these will be the key takeaways for you from this book. While I believe strongly in all of the advice and techniques I have offered, these ten tips carry special weight. They are the core principles on which I founded my consulting business, and I continue to preach them to my clients to this day.

Below, I've referenced the chapters where I introduced these concepts, so you can check back and refresh your memory on the details.

1. **Strategy comes first** *(Chapters 1 and 2)*. Before you can go in search of a new partner, you need to know yourself. The acquisition process should always begin with a company self-examination that leads to a strategic plan for your business. The first step in this process is therefore to develop a practical understanding of where you've been, where you are today, and where you are headed.

2. **Have ONE reason for an acquisition** *(Chapter 3)*. For every acquisition, you should be looking to fill just one specific strategic

need. Trying to meet multiple needs with a single acquisition is likely to result in a solution that fails to fit any of those needs well. By contrast, focusing on one need gives a firm structure to the entire process and ensures clear criteria for your selection of markets and targets.

3. **Anticipate future demand** *(Chapter 2)*. Your growth depends on meeting the needs of customers that you do not yet have. This means that future demand is even more important than current demand. In conducting your market research, you should invest much of your effort in divining what customers will be looking for in five, ten, or even fifteen years' time. Choosing a market with strong future demand is one of the keys to making a successful acquisition.

4. **Every company is for sale for the right equation** *(Chapters 3, 7, 8, 9, and 10)*. As you can see by how often it is mentioned, this is one of the most important principles underlying the Roadmap approach. The critical distinction here is that "equation" means more than price. It includes everything that might prompt owners to sell their company, and the mix of factors can vary dramatically from situation to situation. Knowing that every company can be bought for the right equation should prompt you to focus on "not-for-sale" companies, dramatically widening the scope of possibilities.

5. **Due diligence and integration planning begin at the start of the acquisition process and continue throughout** *(Chapters 12 and 13)*. Due diligence refers to the gathering of critical information about a company, while integration refers to how that information is used once the acquisition is consummated. From the moment you begin your search, you should be seeking the maximum information possible on your prospects and envisioning how integration will be executed. Once you get to the formal stage of due diligence, you will be mostly confirming what you have already learned. And once

you reach integration, you will already know how the new merged entity should function.

6. **Maintain a Prospect Funnel** *(Chapter 6)*. The Prospect Funnel is the acquisition equivalent to a classic sales funnel. It is based on the principle that you should be considering multiple prospective companies, not just one. As you conduct your research, some prospects are set aside while others are moved further down the funnel. Having multiple prospects means that you always have a backup in case something goes wrong with your initial preference.

7. **Create and involve a multifunctional acquisition team** *(Chapters 4, 5, 6, 8, 9, 10, and 12)*. Buying a company involves multiple skills and multiple perspectives, and your acquisition team should be drawn from the key functional areas of your business. The A-Team helps you develop your prospect and market criteria, filter and prioritize markets and prospects, develop your Negotiation Platform, and perform due diligence and integration. It is essential to assemble the entire A-Team at the beginning and keep its members involved throughout the process.

8. **Choose your market before you select your prospects** *(Chapters 3 and 5)*. Before you search for a potential acquisition, you need to make sure you are in the right market. Markets can be defined geographically, vertically, or any other way that is appropriate for your industry. This principle stems from the demand-driven philosophy of growth. However good the prospect you are looking at, it can serve your purposes only if future customer demand is strong and market conditions are favorable.

9. **Consider using a third-party adviser** *(Chapters 4, 5, 6, 7, 8, 10, and 12)*. A third-party adviser can bring an experienced and objective perspective to the acquisition process. During market and prospect research, such advisers can build connections and elicit information while maintaining your anonymity. They can also handle the delicate moment of first contact with an owner and help guide the negotiation process thereafter.

10. **Valuation is an art, not a science** *(Chapters 9 and 12).* There are many ways to calculate the value of a company, and I recommend using at least three different methods: discounted cash flow, liquidation value, and completed transaction comparables. It's important to show the seller the inputs that you used to arrive at the valuation. Also, helping sellers to find their own valuation expert can demonstrate your commitment to a fair approach and increase the objectivity of the process.

GLOSSARY

Acquisition Agreement
A document to effect legal conveyance of an asset or shares being acquired; essentially a roadmap for all parts of the transaction that reflects the chosen deal structure.

Acquisition Team—External
Advisers outside your business who aid you in the acquisition process; includes investment bankers, legal, accountants, due diligence experts, and M&A consultants.

Acquisition Team—Internal
The team within your company responsible for overseeing the acquisition process; includes the backing of the CEO, an Acquisition Coordinator, and a consensus committee from the functional areas of your business. (Sometimes referred to as the A-Team.)

Asset Purchase
The buyer purchases certain specified assets of the target and may include certain specified liabilities of the target; the target's existence continues following the transaction.

Asset Value
The value of all the assets of a business; a form of valuation.

Baskets
Used to aggregate indemnification claims that, when a certain dollar amount is reached, trigger the indemnification claim.

Beta (β)
A measure of a stock's sensitivity to the movement of the general market (S&P 500).

Cost of Debt
Part of the formula used for calculating WACC; K_d. Cost of Debt $= i * (1 -$ Tax rate)

Cost of Equity
Part of the formula used for calculating WACC; K_e. Cost of Equity $= R_f + \beta(R_m - R_f)$

Criteria
The characteristics developed by a buyer for both markets and prospects in order to evaluate their attractiveness and benchmark markets and evaluate prospects against each other; helps reduce emotion and maintain objectivity.

Discounted Cash Flow (DCF)
A valuation technique considered the most theoretically correct way to think about valuation; concerns the present value of projected free cash flows that most explicitly incorporates the future. DCF = Present value of cash flow + Present value of terminal value

Due Diligence
The investigation and/or audit of a prospect that serves to confirm the material facts with regard to the acquisition; a chance to identify growth opportunities.

Escrow
A percentage of the transaction size that is held in a separate account and paid to the seller after a certain amount of time after closing in order to make sure all claims of the seller are true.

External Growth
Growth through the means of working with another company (such as an acquisition, a joint venture, or a licensing agreement).

First Visit Materials
A presentation to the prospect by the buyer given at the first meeting between the two companies.

Five Forces Analysis
Developed by Michael Porter, this tool forces a company to think about five main marketplace influencers: new entrants, suppliers, customers, substitutes, and competitors.

Free Cash Flow (FCF)
A measure of a company's net increase in operating cash flow (this includes the reduction for interest), less the dividends paid to preferred shareholders, and less expenditures necessary to maintain assets (capital expenditures).

g
The perpetual growth rate of a company; used in terminal value calculation.

Greenfielding
Entering into a new market or product in which a company has no previous experience.

Hart-Scott-Rodino (HSR)
An antitrust law requiring the buyer to notify the U.S. government if an acquisition is above a certain threshold set by the government.

i
Interest, part of the calculation of Cost of Debt in the WACC formula; long-term interest (LTI) divided by long-term debt (LTD).

Indemnification
Provides a means for the buyer to seek recourse against the seller for losses suffered as a result of a violation of the Purchase Agreement; most often used to recoup losses suffered due to breaches of representations and warranties.

Integration
The process by which a newly acquired company is brought into the fold of the buyer.

Introductory Materials
Materials tailored for external growth that are sent to a prospect and delivered prior to a first meeting; these materials introduce the buyer and provide differentiation.

Joint Venture
The cooperation of two businesses in a specific enterprise where they agree to share profit, loss, and control.

Letter of Intent
A document that lays out legal points while marketing the buyer as a potential partner/acquirer; a written "gentleman's agreement."

Market Risk Premium
Used to calculate WACC and Cost of Equity; $R_m - R_f$.

Merger
The sale of a widely held or publicly traded company or a company with dissident stockholders; the target is merged into the buyer and all assets and liabilities of the target become those of the buyer.

"Not-for-Sale" Company
A company that is not advertising itself as "for sale" through traditional channels such as a broker or investment bank; does not necessarily mean that an owner won't sell if contacted proactively by an interested buyer.

Opportunity Matrix
A tool used to determine which markets and types of prospects a buyer may want to target in order to grow the business externally.

Organic Growth
Growing a company internally; for example, adding sales staff, making capital investments, or investing in research and development.

Present Value
The amount that a future sum of money is worth today given a specified rate of return.

Primary Research
Research that is usually performed on the phone or face-to-face with someone knowledgeable about a market or specific company; the knowledgeable individual could be an industry expert, competitor, prospect employee, etc.

Proactive Search
Contacting the owners of companies that meet your acquisition criteria to determine what it would take for them to sell their company to you and convince them that you are the right buyer.

Reactive Search
Responding to notices or information that a company or product line is for sale.

Representations and Warranties
Blanket statements in the acquisition agreement describing essential legal, operational, and financial facts regarding the selling company.

Return on market (R_m)
Part of the formula used to calculate Cost of Equity when calculating WACC; the percent return on the market index. This is the average return of the appropriate public equity index over time, for example, large company stocks or small company stocks over the past eighty years.

Risk-free rate of return (R_f)
Part of the formula used to calculate Cost of Equity when calculating WACC; generally, the rate of return of a twenty-year treasury bond.

Secondary Research
Research that is performed on the Internet or through databases that have already been compiled.

Stock Purchase
A deal structure where the buyer purchases all of the stock of the target from the selling stockholders, often resulting in the target becoming a wholly owned subsidiary of the buyer.

Terminal Value
The value of a business at the end of the projected period. $TV = FCF_{TY}/(WACC - g)$

Trading Comparable
A valuation technique for public companies based on market trading multiples of comparable companies.

Transaction Comparable Analysis
A valuation technique based on multiples paid for comparable companies in sale transactions.

WACC
Weighted Average Cost of Capital; a company's cost of capital that weights each category of capital proportionately minus debt and equity. The formula for calculating WACC is: WACC = (Cost of Equity) (%Equity) + (Cost of Debt) (%Debt)

RESOURCES

HELPFUL INTERNET SITES FOR COMPANY INFORMATION

Note that some of these sites require subscriptions.

Briefing.com: www.briefing.com
Bureau van Dijk: www.bvdep.com
Corporate Financials Online: www.cfonews.com
Dow Jones: www.dowjones.com
Dun & Bradstreet: www.dnb.com
Euronext: https://europeanequities.nyx.com
European Business Register: www.ebr.org
Fredonia Group: www.freedoniagroup.com
Google: www.google.com
Hoover's Online: www.hoovers.com
Kompass: www.kompass.com
LexisNexis: www.lexisnexis.com
Manufacturing.net: www.manufacturing.net
MarketWatch: www.marketwatch.com
McGraw-Hill Companies: www.mcgraw-hill.com

Moody's: www.moodys.com

OneSource: www.onesource.com

PR Newswire: www.prnewswire.com

Researchmag.com: www.advisorone.com

Reuters: www.reuters.com

Thomas Register: www.thomasnet.com

U.S. Securities and Exchange Commission: www.sec.gov

STOCK RESEARCH WEBSITES

CNN Money: www.money.cnn.com

Euronext: https://europeanequities.nyx.com

Financial Times: www.ft.com

Green Money Journal: www.greenmoneyjournal.com

Investor's Business Daily: www.investors.com

London Stock Exchange: www.londonstockexchange.com

Motley Fool: www.fool.com

Perfect Information: www.perfectinfo.com

Reuters: www.reuters.com

SEC Forms and Filings: www.sec.gov/edgar.shtml

Yahoo Finance: http://biz.yahoo.com

Yahoo Finance (France): http://fr.finance.yahoo.com

Yahoo Finance (Germany): http://de.finance.yahoo.com

Yahoo Finance (UK): http://uk.finance.yahoo.com

VALUATION/WACC RESOURCES

Capital IQ: www.capitaliq.com

Harvard Business School (Alpha/Beta Guide): www.library.hbs.edu/guides/alpha/

Ibbotson/Morningstar (Industry Beta calculations): http://corporate.morningstar.com

OneSource: www.onesource.com

S&P Stock Reports: www.standardandpoors.com

ValueLine Survey (Key WACC components for public companies): www
.valueline.com

SUGGESTED READING

Bruner, Robert. *Deals from Hell: M&A Lessons That Rise Above the Ashes*. Hoboken, NJ: John Wiley & Sons, 2005.

Copeland, Tom, et al. *Valuation: Measuring and Managing the Value of Companies*. New York: John Wiley & Sons, 1994.

Evans, Frank C., and David M. Bishop. *Valuation for M&A*. New York: John Wiley & Sons, 2001.

Freund, James C. *Anatomy of a Merger*. New York: Law Journal Seminars Press, 1975.

Harvard Business Review. *Harvard Business Review on Mergers & Acquisitions*. Boston: Harvard Business School Press, 2001.

Jenks, Philip, and Stephen Eckett, eds. *The Global-Investor Book of Investing Rules*. Petersfield, UK: Harriman House Ltd., 2001.

Lajoux, Alexandra Reed, and Charles Elson. *The Art of M&A Due Diligence*. New York: McGraw-Hill, 2000.

Marks, Mitchell Lee, and Phillip H. Mirvis. *Joining Forces: Making One Plus One Equal Three in Mergers, Acquisitions, and Alliances*. San Francisco: Jossey-Bass, 2010.

Rickertsen, Rick. *Buyout: The Insider's Guide to Buying Your Own Company*. New York: AMACOM, 2001.

Rosenbloom, Arthur, ed. *Due Diligence for Global Deal Making*. Princeton, NJ: Bloomberg Press, 2002.

Sherman, Andrew J. *Mergers and Acquisitions from A to Z*, 3rd ed. New York: AMACOM, 2010.

APPENDIX:
SAMPLE LETTER OF INTENT

_____, 20__

John Doe

Jane Doe

Acme, Inc.

_____

_____

Re: ACQUISITION OF ACME, INC.

Mr. and Mrs. Doe:

This letter agreement will confirm our recent discussions regarding the acquisition of all of the capital stock of Acme, Inc. a _____ corporation (the **"Company"**), from _____ and _____ (the **"Sellers"**) by [Client Name] (**"Buyer"**) through its wholly owned subsidiary, Core Company, Inc. (**"CCI,"** and together with Buyer, the **"Buyers"**).

The principal terms and conditions of the proposed acquisition are set forth below.

1. **Purchase Price.** Buyers will acquire the capital stock of the Company for the aggregate potential purchase price of $_____, subject to adjustment as set forth below.

2. **Payment of Purchase Price**. The purchase price will be paid by Buyers as follows:

(a) $_____ shall be paid in cash by wire transfer of funds to the Sellers at the closing (as adjusted (i) downward by the amount of all outstanding funded indebtedness of the Company as of the closing date; and (ii) upward or downward for any Working Capital and cash adjustments described in paragraphs 2(c) and 2(d) below); and

(b) $_____ shall be paid in the form of cash to an escrow fund for two years to partially cover any indemnification obligations of the Sellers for breaches of representations, warranties and covenants or for potential Working Capital adjustments described in Paragraph 5 below, if any; any indemnification claims; and for any future uncollected amounts under recourse leases that were outstanding on the actual closing date; and

(c) The cash portion of the purchase price payable under paragraph (a) above at closing shall be adjusted (i) downward on a dollar-for-dollar basis by the amount, if any, by which the Company's Working Capital, as defined below, on the effective closing date is more than $_____ less than the average of the Company's Working Capital balances at the end of each of the six months ending on the month through which Buyers complete their due diligence; or (ii) upward on a dollar-for-dollar basis by the amount, if any, by which the Company's Working Capital on the effective closing date is more than $_____ more than the average of the Company's Working Capital balances at the end of each of the six months ending on the month through which Buyers complete their due diligence; and

(d) The cash portion of the purchase price payable under paragraph (a) above at closing shall be adjusted (i) downward on a dollar-for-dollar basis by the amount, if any, by which the Company's cash on the effective closing date, as adjusted for any transactions outside the ordinary course of the Sellers' business between the effective closing date and the actual closing date, is less than $_____; or (ii) upward on a dollar-for-dollar basis by the amount, if any, by which the Company's cash on the effective closing date, as adjusted for any transactions outside the ordinary course of the Sellers' business between the effective closing date and the actual closing date, is more than $_____.

(e) For the purpose of this letter, **"Working Capital"** shall mean the difference between the Company's (i) current assets (excluding cash and amounts due from shareholders) and (ii) current liabilities (excluding the current portion of any funded indebtedness), as adjusted at closing and as adjusted for other non-recurring items between the effective date and the closing date, but each as calculated in accordance with GAAP and consistent with prior periods.

(f) For the purpose of this letter, **"Funded Indebtedness"** shall mean all (i) indebtedness of the Company for borrowed money or other interest-bearing indebtedness, (ii) capital lease obligations that are accrued or required to be accrued under GAAP, (iii) obligations to pay the deferred purchase or acquisition price for goods or services or businesses acquired by the Company that are accrued or required to be accrued under GAAP, other than trade accounts payable or accrued expenses in the ordinary course of business on no more than ninety (90)–day payment terms or other indebtedness of the Company under extended credit terms of more than thirty (30) days from manufacturers provided to the Company, (iv) indebtedness of others guaranteed by the Company or secured by an encumbrance on any of the Company's assets; (v) the long-term portion of any deferred revenue of the Company not included in Working Capital (the current portion of deferred revenue included in Working Capital shall not be treated as Funded Indebtedness); (vi) floor planning payments in excess of ninety (90) days prior to the Effective Date; or (vii) any receivables or payables owed by the Company to the Sellers.

3. **Structure of the Transaction.** As soon as practical after acceptance of this letter, Buyers will in good faith:

(a) Conduct due diligence on the stock, assets, operations, and financial condition of the Company, with such due diligence to be completed no later than sixty (60) days from acceptance of this letter.

(b) If the results of our due diligence are satisfactory to us, Buyers will in good faith negotiate a definitive stock purchase agreement pursuant to which Buyers will acquire all of the capital stock of the Company from the Sellers pursuant to the above arrangement. It is our intent to sign the definitive agreement on a date mutually agreed upon by the parties hereto but not later than _____, 20__ (the **"closing date"**), [and close effective as of _____, 20__ (the **"effective closing date"**)]. The definitive agreement shall contain, among other items:

(i) representations, warranties, and covenants typical for transactions of this type for both the Sellers and the Buyers; and

(ii) reasonable indemnification from the Sellers to the Buyers and from the Buyers to the Sellers relating to breaches of representations, warranties, and covenants; and

(iii) conditions precedent to each party's obligation to close the transaction; and

(iv) such other terms as Buyers may deem appropriate, based on their due diligence investigation, or are reasonable and customary in transactions of this type and are requested by the Sellers.

4. Conditions to Buyers' Obligations. Buyers' agreement to proceed with the acquisition is subject to the following conditions precedent:

(a) <u>Due Diligence</u>. Buyers shall have completed due diligence on the Company and the operations and future projections of the Company to their satisfaction, including, but not limited to:

(i) *No Litigation.* Buyers shall have determined that there are no actions or proceedings, pending or threatened, in or before any court or governmental body that seek to restrain, prohibit, or invalidate or otherwise interfere with the transaction, or that allege damages arising from the transaction; and

(ii) *No Adverse Change.* Buyers shall have determined that there has been no material adverse change or development concerning the financial condition, earnings prospects, or assets of the Company from that presented to us, and the Company's operations shall continue to have been operated in the ordinary course of business; and

(iii) *Licenses and Contracts.* Buyers shall have determined that the Company has all necessary franchises, trademarks, trade names, licenses, and contracts necessary to own and operate the Company's operations as they are now owned and operated, and all of such licenses, contracts, and agreements shall (A) be in full force and effect without violation by the Company in any material respect, (B) remain in full force and effect immediately following the closing, and (C) be on terms reasonably satisfactory to Buyers; and

(iv) *Suppliers, Customers, and Employees.* Buyers shall have determined from their discussions with the key suppliers, customers, and employees of the Company that the Company's relationships with such firms or individuals are satisfactory and that no material adverse impact to such relationships will result from the sale. Buyers shall obtain the Company's consent prior to initiating such discussions, which consent shall not be unreasonably withheld provided, however, that a representative of the Company shall have the right to participate in such discussions.

(b) <u>No Changes in Payments</u>. Since [date], the Company shall have made no dividends or other distributions to the

Sellers other than in the normal course of business consistent with past practice.

(c) Employment.

(i) John Doe ("**Manager**") shall resign from the Company as of the effective closing date but will remain available on a consulting basis for ninety (90) days to facilitate the transition of the business to the Buyers.

(ii) Jane Doe ("**Doe**") shall agree to continue to remain as an employee of the Company with the title of President following the closing. Doe shall enter into a customary two-year executive agreement with the Company that will contain a surviving three-year non-competition covenant. The executive agreement will pay Doe a base salary of $_____ per year, and will entitle Doe to be eligible for an annual bonus of up to fifty percent (50%) of the base salary commencing with Buyers' fiscal year beginning _____ provided that Doe shall also be eligible for a pro rata portion of such annual bonus for the fiscal year ending _____, which pro rata bonus shall be guaranteed (i.e., pro rated from the effective closing date through the remainder of fiscal year _____). Doe will also receive a car allowance of $_____ per month. Doe will also be eligible for stock options and overachievement bonuses starting with her first full fiscal year with Buyers as determined by the Board of Directors of Buyers. Severance and other terms of the executive agreement will be as customary for other executives of Buyers in similar positions.

(d) Non-compete Covenant. The Stock Purchase Agreement will contain a four-year non-competition covenant, and $_____ of the purchase price will be allocated to the non-competition covenant.

(e) Payment of Indebtedness. All funded indebtedness of the Company (except for trade payables outstanding on ninety (90)–day or less payment terms) shall be paid by the Sellers on, or prior to, the closing date or the cash portion of the purchase price will be reduced by the amount of such funded indebtedness. All liens on the shares or assets of the Company shall have been released on, or prior to, the closing date.

(f) Building Leases. Buyers shall enter into a new lease with Sellers for the 20,000 square feet currently occupied by the Company at its present facility in _____, [State] for an initial five-year term. The [State] lease shall contain financial terms substantially similar to the current lease, and shall include other terms as are customary in a lease of this type.

(g) <u>No Adverse Disclosure or Change</u>. There will be no material adverse event or change in the Company's business position, outlook, or potential.

(h) <u>Personal Vehicles and Other Personal Assets</u>. All personal vehicles (including the related debt) and other personal assets will be taken out of the business by the Sellers prior to the closing date.

5. **Closing Balance Sheet Review**. Buyers will prepare a closing balance sheet, cash and Working Capital analysis as of the effective closing date within one hundred eighty (180) days following the closing date. In the event the calculation of cash or Working Capital is less than the preliminary cash or Working Capital determined as of the closing date, Buyers may collect such difference from the escrow fund, or collect such difference from the Sellers, subject to the cash or Working Capital allowances referenced in Paragraphs 2(c) and 2(d). If the results of this analysis are disputed by the Sellers, Buyers will retain an independent accounting firm to provide a review of the results. If this review differs by less than ten percent (10%) of Buyers' analysis, the Sellers will reimburse Buyers for the expense of such independent accounting firm.

6. **Access**. Upon your acceptance of this letter, the Sellers and the Company will permit representatives of Buyers access upon reasonable notice to the Company's books and records, facilities, key personnel, and independent accountants (including access to the work papers of the Company's independent accountants) in connection with its due diligence review of the Company, which review will be completed as expeditiously as possible.

7. **No Shop; Exclusivity; Confidentiality**. The Sellers and the Company each agree that following the acceptance of this letter and prior to the first to occur of (i) the termination by Buyers of their due diligence without a decision to proceed to negotiate a definitive stock purchase agreement, or (ii) sixty (60) days from the acceptance of this letter neither the Sellers nor the Company shall offer to sell, entertain, or initiate discussion of any offer to sell, or solicit any proposals regarding the sale of, all or any part of the stock or assets of the Company with any party other than Buyers. The parties hereto, and

their representatives, agree that this letter and the transactions contemplated by this letter and the information provided pursuant to this letter shall remain in strict confidence and that all proprietary information obtained by either party or their representatives will be kept confidential, except for any information that is now or hereafter available to the public.

8. **Non-binding Effect**. Except for the provisions of Paragraphs 7 and 9 hereof, which shall be binding on the parties to this letter, this letter of intent shall represent the present intentions of the parties only and shall not be binding until such time, if ever, that the parties negotiate, execute, and deliver a stock purchase agreement reasonably acceptable to the parties.

9. **Expenses**. Each of the parties hereto agrees to bear its own transaction expenses and brokerage fees in connection with the transactions contemplated hereby. The Sellers shall bear all of the Company's legal and other transaction expenses associated with the transactions contemplated hereby.

10. **Miscellaneous**. Please signify your acceptance of, and your agreement to be bound by the terms hereof, by executing one copy of this letter and returning it to us. **THIS AGREEMENT MAY BE EXECUTED IN COUNTERPARTS AND SHALL BE GOVERNED BY _____ LAW.** Copies of original signatures sent by facsimile transmission shall be binding as evidence of such acceptance and agreement. This letter of intent supersedes all prior letters of intent, correspondence, or other arrangements between the Company, the Sellers, and the Buyers with respect to the transactions contemplated by this letter.

[THIS SPACE INTENTIONALLY LEFT BLANK]

If you are in agreement with the terms of this letter, and desire to proceed with the transaction on that basis, please sign the enclosed duplicate of this letter in the space provided and return it to us.

Very truly yours,

[CLIENT NAME]

By: _____

    Name: _____

    Title: _____

AGREED AND ACCEPTED

ACME, INC.   Date: _____

By: _____

    Name: _____

    Title: _____

_____   Date: _____

Jane Doe

_____   Date: _____

John Doe

INDEX